EDGAR WAYBURN: *Redwoods and rhododendron*

This is the land of the last redwoods.

JAMES ROSE: *Sunset, Gold Bluffs beach*

*This is the last of an ancient race,
in a land of majestic forms . . .*

MARTIN LITTON: *Redwood Creek forest*

JAMES ROSE: *Stream pattern, Redwood Creek*

GORDON ROBINSON: *Roosevelt elk, Gold Bluffs meadow*

*. . . a land of serenity and grace,
evocative of a past long forgotten*

*. . . a land of old beginnings, ongoing
until man came with the power to destroy
or to spare.*

JAMES ROSE: *Morning, Elam Creek*

THE LAST REDWOODS
and the Parkland of Redwood Creek

SIERRA CLUB · BALLANTINE BOOKS

JAMES ROSE: *Lower Redwood Creek*

Text *by* FRANÇOIS LEYDET

Photographs *by* JAMES ROSE *and others*

Introduction *by* EDGAR *and* PEGGY WAYBURN

[9

THE SIERRA CLUB, founded in 1892 by John Muir, has devoted itself to the study and protection of national scenic resources, particularly those of mountain regions. All Sierra Club publications are part of the nonprofit effort the club carries on as a public trust. The club is affiliated with the International Union for Conservation, the Natural Resources Council of America, the Conservation Foundation, and the Federation of Western Outdoor Clubs. The club began in California and now has chapters in all parts of the United States, including Alaska and Hawaii. *Main Office:* Mills Tower, San Francisco. *Other offices:* 15 East 53rd Street, New York; 235 Massachusetts Avenue, N.E., Washington, D.C.; 427 West 5th Street, Los Angeles; 111D Harvard Drive, S.E., Albuquerque; 4535½ University Way, N.E., Seattle; and Anchorage, Alaska.

Publisher's note: The text of this book has been set in Fairfield, the display type in Centaur, by Gillick Printing, Inc., in Berkeley, California. The book was printed on Consolidated Durado, Dull Coated, by Case-Hoyt Printers in Rochester, New York, and bound in Permalin by A. Horowitz and Son in Clifton, New Jersey.

The photograph on the front cover was taken by James Rose in Redwood Creek forest, in an area logged in 1967. The back cover photograph, also by James Rose, depicts clean logging at North Fork, Lost Man Creek.

The lines that appear on page 16 are copyright © 1954 by John Stewart Collis, reprinted from *The Triumph of the Tree* by John Stewart Collis, published by William Sloane Associates, William Morrow and Company, Inc. The excerpt on pages 46 and 48 is copyright 1951 by Loren Eiseley and reprinted from *The Immense Journey* by Loren Eiseley by permission of Random House, Inc. The lines on page 50 are © copyright 1963 by Garth Jeffers and Donnan Jeffers, reprinted from *The Beginning and the End and Other Poems* by Robinson Jeffers by permission of Random House, Inc.

PUBLISHER'S NOTE

IN 1912, E. C. Williams, last of the original quartet which started making red-wood lumber commercially, reminisced in the *Mendocino Beacon* about his first prospecting for timber in the dark Sequoia wilderness of California's north-ern coast in 1850. It was spring as he took a rough redwood canoe up the Big River, bank full, "its slight ripples meeting the verdure of the shore, the tall red-woods with their great symmetrical trunks traveling toward the skies; with the bright colors of the rhododendrons profusely scattered over the hills forming the background, the clear blue sky above reflected in the placid river and over all the hush and solitude of the primeval forest — all combining to impress upon our minds the beauty and truth [in] Bryant's *Thanatopsis,* 'The groves were God's first temples.' "

Recalling the scene, he added, "I cannot but regret the part it appeared neces-sary for me to enact in what now looks like a desecration."

There are no places left where one can duplicate Williams's experience of 1850. Logging began first along the banks which bore the stateliest stands of tim-ber and which were most accessible. And logging has continued throughout the region for 120 years. Today, a traveler flying low over the Coast Range sees a vast panorama of cut-over land: denuded hillsides are interlaced with logging roads; where great forests were once silhouetted against the sky, there is now an occasional tall snag to mark their height; here and there are small islands of rich dark green, the last scraps of the primeval forest.

The best estimates we have indicate that the original coastal redwood forests covered about two million acres along the northern California coast in 1830. Close to 90 out of every 100 acres has now been logged or burned, cleared for pasture, built on, paved over for highways or parking lots, or converted to commercial tree farms which, it is hoped, will keep on growing one kind of tree or another. The primeval redwood forests are almost gone; less than four percent have been set aside in public ownership.

What has happened to these great trees epitomizes the fate of most of our American forests. As Stewart Udall noted in the foreword to the original edition of *The Last Redwoods,* we are "a nation of woodsmen who made Paul Bunyan a national folklore hero." The early settlers assumed ownership of a continent full of the most magnificent forests on the planet. The Pilgrims, the saying goes, fell first onto their knees and then onto the Indians. They fell next onto the forests — and we have been at war with our trees ever since. We conquered first (and obliterated) the great white pines of New England and the long-leafed yellow pines of the southern seaboard. Cutting moved westward with the pioneers; the

EDGAR WAYBURN: *Count's Hill Prairie, upper Redwood Creek*

hardwood forests made way for corn fields; the pines and firs of Michigan and Minnesota and Wisconsin went down, and the conifers of Mississippi and Texas; and still we logged on. We were slowed only by the sea and by the size and profuseness of our far western forests.

On a conservative estimate, we have sent over half of our forests up in smoke. The rest we have considered as a commodity, useful as timber and wood products, and valuable in terms of dollars. We came late to the realization that these forests were not limitless, and that we needed to treat them with care if they were to survive our onslaught. We came even later to the understanding that some of our forests should not be cut at all — that they might have other and greater value than being made into grape stakes, shingles, sidings, coffins, patio furniture, doghouses and cigar boxes.

The overwhelming popular support for a Redwood National Park shows that the majority of Americans have come to share this view. Unfortunately, the park set up by the 91st Congress is less than the public — and the redwoods — deserve. Its size was determined by dollars and politics, and not by the conservation opportunity that was there in 1968. Of the 33,000 acres of primeval forest that could have been acquired, only 11,000 acres were included in the park.

In 1971, the conservation opportunity is still there—though it is being diminished daily by the logging that goes on relentlessly. (At the present rate of cutting, the bulk of the primeval forests remaining in private ownership will be "harvested" about a decade from now.) There are new bills in Congress to redraw the boundaries of the park. If we act with vision and boldness, we can still achieve a great Redwood National Park.

This book, then, has a newer and broader meaning than *The Last Redwoods* published in 1963. It remains, like that book, a requiem for what we could have saved and didn't. It remains a salute to the men of vision and generosity who worked so long and hard to save what has been saved of a superb natural heritage. It is also a celebration of a major conservation achievement, realization of a dream of many men, the establishment of a Redwood National Park.

Most importantly, however, this book is a renewed and urgent plea to keep up the fight for the redwoods while there is still a chance to fight for them. It is a challenge to a generation that will be remembered for its extraordinary technological achievements and, we hope, for recognizing its ecological responsibility to the earth and to those that follow. What we save of the redwoods, it should be recalled, will be not only for us, but for the untold numbers to come who will deserve some chance to experience the wonder and beauty that Williams knew such a short time ago.

—EDGAR WAYBURN
Past President of the Sierra Club

ACKNOWLEDGMENTS

LIKE THE REDWOODS it portrays, this book is the end product of the interaction and cooperation of many forces — in this case people of varying backgrounds and expertise. We are grateful to them all.

The text is based on *The Last Redwoods,* published by the Sierra Club in 1963. Particular thanks are due to Philip Hyde and François Leydet, respectively the photographer and the author of that book, and to others who helped in the preparation and scrutiny of the original text: to Mrs. Frances Purser, Librarian of the Humboldt County Collection in the Library of Humboldt State College; to Josephine Moore, Plumas County Librarian; to George Marshall, who gave constant support to the project and who helped assess material in the Huntington Library; to Russell D. Butcher for much of the preliminary research; to Glen N. Jones, former Supervisor of Prairie Creek Redwoods State Park; to Carl Anderson of California's Division of Beaches and Parks; to Ted Hatzimanolis, U.S. Forest Service, Requa; to Professor Paul Zinke, School of Forestry, University of California, Berkeley; and to David E. Pesonen and David Brower.

Additional thanks go to those who helped in preparing this present volume: J. Michael McCloskey, Conservation Director of the Sierra Club, has updated the original text in close cooperation with François Leydet. Alfred Marty has prepared new maps showing the Redwood National Park. The botanist John Thomas Howell has checked the species list at the end of the book. Dr. Edgar Wayburn, leader of the Sierra Club's redwood campaign, has revised the Publisher's Note, which he signed as president of the Sierra Club in 1963. His wife, Peggy Wayburn, has prepared a new chapter on the parkland of Redwood Creek; together they have written a new introduction. Most of the color photographs are by James Rose, who was still in his teens when he started taking them, and who made it a personal project not only to document the redwoods, but to become an expert on the area and on the strategy of saving it.

A special kind of gratitude is owed Martin Litton, whose photographs in the original edition had to be anonymous. He carries with him a pilot's-eye view of the state of California, among many places, and early noted on this cerebral map the magnificent forest of Redwood Creek. Throughout the struggle to establish the national park, and in the continuing struggle to complete it, he provided not only information, but also advice, stimulation, and a feeling of urgency. He piloted the authors — as well as photographers, members of the Administration and of the Congress — on numerous aerial trips over the redwood region, providing a fund of information and on-the-spot observations from which more was learned than could be gathered in weeks of research.

We are grateful to all who submitted photographs for this edition, whether or not they were used. We also appreciate the work of David Brower, Kenneth Brower, and Peggy Wayburn, who are largely responsible for the layout and editing of the book.

We regret that so many of the photographs are of beautiful places that no longer exist, and we hope that all readers will join in preventing the destruction of the beautiful places that still remain.

— AUGUST FRUGÉ, *Chairman, Publications Committee*

The existence of trees was a prerequisite of conceptual thought. It was the tree that gave the hand to life. It was the tree that promoted the upright posture. It was the tree that made sight dominant over smell. Must we not say that it was the tree that gave man to life? Anyway, it was under the auspices of those ancient boughs that he appeared. And having appeared, he was destined to interfere with the Order of Nature. The very forests were doomed.
— JOHN STEWART COLLIS, The Triumph of the Tree

CONTENTS

All the photographs in this book, except those on pages 31, 61, 110, 122, and 134, were taken in the Redwood Creek area. Photographs on pages 12, 26, 39, 47, 52, 64, 136, and 155 show areas outside present park boundaries which may already have been logged.

JAMES ROSE: *Detail, forest floor, lower Redwood Creek*

INTRODUCTION

Sixth in the Sierra Club's Exhibit Format series, *The Last Redwoods* with text by François Leydet and photographs by Philip Hyde, was first published in 1963. Like the earlier books, it was an eloquent argument for a vanishing scenic resource, in this case an incomparable forest. It was also the most comprehensive documentary on the redwoods published up to that time. Most important, *The Last Redwoods* was conceived and produced with a deliberate purpose: it was meant to alert the public to the perilous situation of the coastal redwoods, which so many people thought were saved. And it was the opening salvo in the Sierra Club's battle to rescue what could still be rescued of the primeval redwood forest.

The club's interest in the redwoods was not new. In 1895, Professor William R. Dudley, an early member, pleaded the cause of *Sequoia sempervirens* in the Sierra Club Bulletin. He urged the "immediate establishment of several redwood parks, under the control of the United States government." At that time, there was a chance to save the redwoods simply and economically, since many forests were still in federal ownership. But Dudley's plea went unheeded. A few years after his article appeared, the last redwood forest lands were allowed to slip from public into private ownership. After the turn of the century, the acquisition of redwoods for public parks necessarily meant the buying back of private property — on the owner's terms.

For several decades, the Sierra Club played largely a supportive role in saving the redwoods, backing the early efforts of the Sempervirens Club and later the Save-the-Redwoods League and the state of California in their programs to establish redwood state parks. The major energies of the club were consumed in conservation campaigns for Yosemite, Mount Rainier, and Sequoia and Kings Canyon National Parks.

In the 1950's, however, public attention — and the club's — was focused on the redwoods by a series of disturbing events. There was the disastrous 1955 flood at Bull Creek, which demonstrated dramatically the need for complete watershed protection if the existing redwood parks were to survive. There was the devastating routing of a freeway through some of the most superb "saved" redwood groves in Humboldt Redwoods State Park, and the threat of similar destruction in Jedediah Smith and Prairie Creek State Parks. And in the early 1960's, there was the grim roadside exhibit of "clean logging" of redwoods along Highway 101 just outside Prairie Creek State Park, which gave painful evidence of what redwood "tree-farming" meant. Clearly, it was time for action.

The state of California and the Save-the-Redwoods League had done a tremendous job in setting aside some of the finest primeval groves in 28 redwood state

JAMES ROSE: *Ridgetop forest above Redwood Creek; elevation approximately 1,100 feet*

parks. But some of these parks were see-through roadside strips and others were almost as tall as they were wide. No state park was adequate to preserve the species and to accommodate the public. The state had neither the means nor the facilities to acquire an area that could tell the redwood story from sea to mountaintop, large enough to insure watershed protection and to survive heavy recreational use. The time had come when the federal government — which had allowed the redwoods to slip through its fingers so long ago — would have to act to reacquire enough of the original primeval forest to make a great Redwood National Park. The wealthiest nation in the world, able to afford billions of dollars to put man into space, could certainly afford it.

The Sierra Club went to work. Along with publishing *The Last Redwoods,* the club made the establishment of a Redwood National Park a top priority.

At the Biennial Wilderness Conference, sponsored by the club in 1963, Secretary of the Interior Stewart L. Udall announced his intention to see such a park created. The National Park Service, with a grant from the National Geographic Society, was already engaged in a field study to identify the park possibilities still remaining in the redwood region. (It is worth noting that, after 115 years of logging, good possibilities did remain — a measure of the prodigious primeval forest that once was there.)

The study, made public in September, 1964, was called simply *The Redwoods.* It recommended a 54,000 acre Redwood National Park at Redwood Creek — and documented the reasons why. The club concurred, but urged that a larger, more significant portion of Redwood Creek be included in a 90,000 acre park.

Traditionally, the establishment of a national park has taken 15 to 25 years. In the case of the redwoods, it was plain that the country could not afford to wait that long. The forests of Redwood Creek were being logged while the Park Service studied them. Logging continued there after the park recommendations were made public. While the pros and cons were aired from Capitol Hill to Crescent City, the great trees fell ever faster. The chance for a major park diminished every day. Time, sometimes the great ally, was the great enemy in the fight for the redwoods. The Sierra Club mounted one of the most intensive conservation campaigns in its history, and one of the most difficult.

The Administration, ignoring the recommendations of its own Park Service study team experts, turned to a different site, Mill Creek in Del Norte County, as its choice for the redwood park. (Mill Creek was superb, but far too small an area, the club felt, to survive as a heavily visited National Park.) Formidable opposition to any sizable national park grew in the lumber industry, which had dominated the redwood region so long.

Despite this opposition, widespread and enthusiastic support developed for the 90,000 acre park on Redwood Creek. In the House of Representatives, Jeffrey Cohelan and John P. Saylor — joined by a record number of Congressmen from Maine to Hawaii — championed the club's proposal. In the Senate, after long and

JAMES ROSE: *Old Bald Hills Road*

careful study, Senators Thomas H. Kuchel and Henry M. Jackson supported the same area. Conservation groups across the country joined forces with the club.

The redwoods battle turned out to be one of the most dramatic on record. No park proposal, Director of the National Park Service George Hartzog noted, ever occasioned a greater flood of letters pro and con. In the redwood region, families were split over the park idea, friendships were made and broken, and political careers won and lost.

The trees themselves inspired strong emotional feelings on both sides. More profoundly, certain fundamental — and controversial — issues were involved. When should private ownership give way to the broader public good? Who should decide this, Congress or the local community? Assuming that economically productive private land must be publically acquired, how could this best be done? Should the park potential of a unique area be destroyed even while Congress was considering ways to save it? (Congress itself answered this midway in the battle by declaring an unprecedented moratorium on logging in certain areas proposed for inclusion in the national park.)

There was also the question of the economic impact of a national park on the redwood region. The timber industry predicted ruin. Conservationists, and many economists, believed a national park would provide greatly needed economic diversity to a depressed, single-industry area.

In view of the complexity of issues and the fierce emotions involved, the battle was surprisingly brief — four fiery years. Reflecting the public's feeling for the redwoods, the bill for a 58,000 acre Redwood National Park (which included three state parks) passed the Senate unanimously — and the House by 327 to 1. On October 2, 1968, President Johnson signed it into law.

Though not optimum, the legislation gained a certain reprieve for the redwoods. It recognized that areas of superlative beauty should belong to all the people, and should not be exploited for the profit of a few. It confirmed the use of federal funds to purchase such areas — in effect, recognizing that parks are as valuable as freeways. It accepted the fact that the government must pay a fair price for private land. It set up machinery for prompt acquisition of land for public use. And it was an object lesson in demonstrating that subsequent generations may have to pay dearly for the mistakes of their forefathers.

Unquestionably, *The Last Redwoods* played a significant role in gaining the Redwood National Park. At the same time, and understandably, the book became and remained a target of criticism from the redwood industry.

Perhaps because it was not easy to fault its contents, critics attacked the title as unfair. There will always be redwoods, they argued. Obviously, the Sierra Club knew that young redwoods can sprout from the stumps of old giants. Just as obviously, the club thought, the title of *The Last Redwoods* did not refer to stump sprouts and seedlings that would grow for a few years and then be cut for pulp or plywood. The title referred to a once-widespread genus that now survives in its last redoubt along the north coast of California. It referred to the last patches of

JAMES ROSE: *Lost Man Creek forest*

a superb primeval forest that managed to live on for millions of years until the advent of modern man.

The title is still apt, and poignantly so, six years after the first edition of *The Last Redwoods* was published. During those years while a park was being won, thousands of acres of superb forest were denuded, gutted, and scraped bare, leaving only the great stumps standing. "Clean logging," as it is called in the redwood region, is the accepted scientific modern method; it is followed by reseeding and, hopefully, by good regeneration of trees that can be cut once more. But whatever it is called and however scientifically it is defended, clean logging has the same wounding impact on a redwood forest as an enormous natural catastrophe — as a massive avalanche or earthquake. The forest can survive such a wound when the wound is small. But practiced on a vast scale, clean logging — no matter what kind of regeneration may follow it — will inevitably and irrevocably change the character of the land, the streams, the plants, the animals, and the beauty of the redwood region. The industry has made it clear just how vast the scale will be: commercial logging will stop only at park boundaries.

These boundaries are by no means adequate. The $92,000,000 invested by Congress in a Redwood National Park could only buy so much. More of the remaining primeval forest was left out than was taken in. Much of the unbroken sweep of forest "lawn" of Redwood Creek and the small exquisite watershed of Skunk Cabbage Creek were necessarily omitted, but with the hope that they could one day soon be acquired. And the day must come soon.

Since the beginning of 1969 new logging roads have been slashed into the forests of Skunk Cabbage Creek, and the bulldozers and chain saws are busily at work. Towering trees, among the most magnificent left in the world, are falling in many acres of this forest. Logging is already moving on an increasing scale into the still unacquired forests above the gorgeous Emerald Mile of Redwood Creek. If these are cut, a narrow line of trees within the park will stand in isolation along a river running thick with eroded topsoil. How long this fragile wall will last is anybody's guess, since unprotected redwoods are highly susceptible to storms and floods; they cannot stand alone.

It may cost the country more money — the price, say, of a few miles of freeway — to save what should still be saved. And continuing the battle after a partial victory will not be easy. But it makes economic sense to buy what is needed to protect a major investment; it makes more sense to buy it soon, before prices escalate even higher and while the forests still stand.

This new edition of *The Last Redwoods,* with François Leydet's text updated, adds fresh material on the parklands of Redwood Creek and the park fight. The beautiful new color photographs of the Redwood Creek area — site of the greatest remaining park opportunity — are largely by James Rose. The book still has much work to do. It must alert the American public once again to the plight of the earth's greatest forest. It must make painfully clear that this is truly the last chance to save the last redwoods.   — EDGAR AND PEGGY WAYBURN

JAMES ROSE: *Going . . . gone? Skunk Cabbage Creek forest*

1 . LIFE OF AN IMMORTAL

CRADLED in its moist bed of humus, the seed lay waiting. It was no bigger than the head of a match — a mere speck of vegetable matter. Yet locked within its tiny body were potent secrets: the secret of life, of a life force so determined that it might last to challenge the laws of mortality; and the secrets of growth — of growth so patient, so steady, so resourceful and relentless that it might some-day tower over all other living things.

These secrets, coded in its genes, the seed had inherited from its parent. That great tree, whose bole soared skyward some 100 feet away, was justifying its name of *Sequoia sempervirens* — ever-living Sequoia. For it had sprouted at the time when, in far-off Mesopotamia, Hammurabi was founding the Babylonian empire. By now Babylon had crumbled, and Hannibal of Carthage was leading his ele-phants across the Alps to throw the Roman Senate into panic. And still this hoary coast redwood stood, having filtered the sun and fogs of 1900 summers through its branches, having drunk the rains of 1900 winters through its roots.

In its genes, then, the seed had the potential to emulate its parent. But whether it would, in fact, do so depended on more than heredity. This, luck would decide. Already, the seed had twice been blessed with luck. First it had been born viable, endowed with the spark of life. Of the thousands of seeds scat-tered the past winter by the parent tree, only a fourth or a third had been so endowed. Then, when the seed was released from its thimble-sized cone two hundred feet aloft among its parent's branches, the whims of air currents had chanced to deposit it at a spot on the forest floor where, when the time came, it could take root.

It did not have too long to wait. The warmth and dampness of the soil quick-ened its urge for life. Its outer covering split. Down went a tiny root; up into the light burst a frail opening shoot.

Fragile though it was, the seedling from the first had all the beauty of its race. It grew straight and graceful. Its reddish-brown trunk was evenly wreathed with branches clad in a lovely foliage rather like a hemlock's. The twin-ranked leaves, dark green and glistening above, delicately silvered with lines of stomata below, grew in flat sprays that spread daintily outward.

The young tree's guardsman-straight stance had a more than aesthetic pur-pose; its unwavering aim was to grow up, up, up — up toward that narrow patch of sky that rent the canopy formed by the crowns of its elders, up into the life-giving light. It could afford to waste neither energy nor time in any deviation from its vertical surge, for it had competitors, and laggards would be crowded out.

This battle for supremacy and survival, obvious out in the open, was waged simultaneously on another front — underground. There, in the dark, its roots groped outward, vying with others for water and nutrients of the soil. A redwood sends out a wide-spreading net of shallow roots which serve both to nourish and support it, a system which in a mature tree may extend 40 to 50 feet away from its base, at four to six feet below the surface of the ground.

Over the decades, the sapling struggled on, fighting to maintain its claim for light and air and food against those of neighbors of its own and other generations. Did the life force flow just a whit more strongly within it than within its competitors? Was the particular patch of soil from which it drew its sustenance just a fraction more fertile? Was the half-light of the forest just a shade brighter upon it? Whatever the reason, it, and a few others, became established and thrived. The rest, weaker or less lucky, did not.

Year by year, our tree grew a little thicker and taller. Water and nutrient salts coursed up its trunk through the outer ring of yellow sapwood, were transformed in the leaves by photosynthesis into carbohydrates, which in turn passed down the sieve-like tubes of the inner bark to be used for the tree's growth. Every year, the soft, protoplasm-filled inner cells of the cambium layer of living sapwood toughened and hardened, and a new band of red heartwood surrounded the old, forming what in cross section would appear as another ring.

The annual increase in height amounted only to inches — in diameter, to fractions of an inch. But by the time a young man of Nazareth began to teach his parables, our tree stood 100 feet tall and three feet through at the base. It had lost its early Christmas tree look; slightly fluted like an Ionic column, the trunk rose bare of branches for half its height. The tree by now had passed the 200-year mark. But at an age that in many species would be venerable, it was a mere adolescent.

Two more centuries passed. Safely over the continuing crisis of infancy and childhood, the tree had in those years more than doubled its height and girth. The most dramatic event in its life had been an unusually violent lightning storm, in which a bolt had exploded in the crown of the parent tree, setting it ablaze. The fire had flickered and smouldered for days, and by the time it had burned itself out the old giant was fatally weakened. Occasional windstorms hit with hurricane force, and a few of the more-exposed veterans came crashing down. In one of these storms the parent tree was toppled.

Presently our young tree met with a new experience. While the first serious irruptions of Germanic tribes into the Roman Empire were beginning, soon to wax into a flood, forces of a different kind were in motion out over the Pacific. A great circling mass of air, heavily laden with rain clouds, began to spiral eastwards, towards the coast of what white men (who had yet to dream of America, let alone a sequoia) would one day call northern California. When the clouds hit the coastal ranges they opened up. For days, for a week, for a month the deluge raged unabated.

At the foot of a steep forested slope, our tree stood on the edge of a flat, a

HOWARD KING: *Prairie Creek forest*

ANN ADAMS: *Streamside, Fern Canyon*

ANN ADAMS: *Spring blossoms, Mill Creek*

high river bench built up by past floods. Now, as the storm continued, the river once again overtopped its banks. Throughout its watershed, swollen creeks collected the runoff from saturated hillsides and added their loads to its stream. Up the trunks of the redwoods in the flat the river's waters rose, thick and soupy with silt.

Finally the storm played itself out, the sun broke through, and the waters receded. But the forest floor was no longer recognizable. In place of the green carpet of fern and oxalis and moss there stretched a flat, bare, gray expanse of silt, What was more, the ground level had risen nearly three feet. Trunks of the bigger trees seemed somewhat shrunken, as now their butt swells were buried in the mud.

For our tree, as for its fellows, this new situation was serious: A redwood's roots have to lie near the surface. But part of the information once locked in the tiny seed was the knowledge of how to cope with just such a challenge as this. The tree began to develop a new and higher root system, and as this took over the job of feeding and supporting it, the older roots were allowed to die.

Another, more serious, crisis overtook the tree a century later. The previous summer had been unusually hot and fog-free; and winter's rains, which in normal years swept in from the ocean in storm after drenching storm, had been intermittent and perfunctory. The drought had persisted through the spring and into this summer. In the evenings, no billows of fog came rolling in over the hills across the river to cool the air and replace the forest's moisture that had evaporated during the day: The fog bank stayed far out to sea, a gray shape crouched on the horizon like a whipped animal. The sun would rise in a clear sky, bake the land all day, and long after it had sunk behind the hills high cirrus clouds shone rose and gold, reflecting its dying rays.

Up in the hills the creeks ran dry, and an unwonted number of deer, bear, and other back-country dwellers crossed the flat to the shrunken river for a drink. The undergrowth was sere and brown, fern fronds snapped off when an animal brushed by them, and the normally sponge-like litter of decaying leaves and needles was light and dry as desert dust.

The fire, when it came, was brutal. Anything young, tender or low-growing was turned to ashes and charcoal. The flames burned deep into the desiccated humus, and in the super-heated air, tongues of fire leaped high up the trunks of the big redwoods. These needed every inch of their thick, asbestos-like bark to protect them from hurt, nor was it always quite enough. The fire was particularly hot on the uphill side of our tree, where debris that had rolled or washed down from the hill lay deep. The bark turned black, then red, then incandescent, and the flames licked at the living sapwood.

Our tree was left with a great, charcoal-covered wound, five feet wide at its base, 15 feet high, shaped like a gothic arch. At ground level a quarter of the sapwood and inner bark essential for life and growth had been destroyed. But though severe, the wound was not fatal, and the tree immediately set about healing the scar.

Inch by inch, year by year, new bark and tissue grew out over the edges of the blackened area. Occasionally a smaller fire, invading the forest, attacked the injured part and interrupted or set back the healing process. But with all the vigor and tenacity that had allowed it first to establish itself against competition, later to adapt to the changes brought about by the flood, the tree persisted in repairing the damage. Within a century, its girdle of bark was restored, and it could return to the century-to-century business of living and growing and producing seed.

By the year 800 A.D., when Charlemagne was crowned Emperor of the Holy Roman Empire, our tree had lived its first millenium. By the time architects and stonemasons and sculptors and glaziers in western Europe were erecting those sublime cathedrals to whose lofty pillared naves redwood groves have been likened, our tree was 1500 years old.

Five times floods had raised the level of the ground. Five times the tree had grown a new system of roots. Twice since that first fierce blaze it had been scarred by fire. Each time it had drawn on its great regenerative power and had closed its wounds. Its huge ribbed trunk, now 15 feet through at the base, rose more than 200 feet straight up to the first downward-sweeping branches. For the next 100 feet it was clad in foliage. This was no thick, bushy spread of needles as might have seemed fitting to a tree of its size, but still the delicate, feminine sprays that adorned it as a sapling — except at the very top, 320 feet up, where its crown broke through the canopy of the forest and where short, awl-shaped needles bore a striking resemblance to those of its cousin, the Big Tree of the Sierra.

Old the tree was — old by human standards, old by the standards of almost all life but its own. And yet it was in the full prime of maturity. On and on it thrived, adding imperceptibly every year to its height and its girth, while men fought crusades and wars, Columbus discovered America, the Pilgrims landed at Plymouth Rock, the Thirteen Colonies broke away from British rule. On and on it lived, while great forests across the continent were being felled by ax and plow.

It was in 1849, the year of the great stampede to the Sierra gold fields, that the tree faced its most deadly challenge. A fire, greater than any that   d suffered and survived, burned through the foot-thick bark, through the sapwoo. and even into the heartwood for a third of its circumference, leaving an enormous 17-foot-wide scar. Worse yet, the fire killed all the roots on one side of the tree.

As time went on, our tree began to list towards the north, the side on which the roots had been killed. The list gradually became more pronounced, until the top was 40 feet north of the base. It seemed that, after more than 2,000 years of life, the tree must shortly fall.

In this extremity, that powerful will to live, the extraordinary secrets of survival that had all been sealed in the little seed came into play in the most amazing way yet. As before, the tree began to heal the scar from each side. But from the side nearest the falling axis, it also started to build out a strong supporting buttress to take over from the now useless roots.

As if it knew that its life was in peril, the tree poured its energy into extending that buttress, pushing it forward half an inch a year — far faster than it was increasing its girth in any other direction. A race was on between the tree and the weather: Could the buttress be built out far enough to give it firm support before a major storm could upset it?

Ten, twenty, fifty, a hundred years rolled by, and still our tree stood firm. The buttress now projected four feet; as every winter struck, it had advanced a little farther towards the north, giving the leaning tree that much more support. Then came the winter of 1955.

Just before the end of the year, a storm of epic proportions swirled in from the ocean — a storm that was to cause landslides, raging floods and major devastation throughout northern California. For days the rain came down in torrents; it poured off the saturated hillside behind the tree into the flat. The soil around the tree became soft, sodden, boggy. With no firm ground under it, the buttress no longer could hold the tree's 1,000 tons.

The end came in the early hours of the morning of December 26th. Slowly at first, the lofty trunk leaned farther out of plumb. There was a tearing sound, as roots parted under the strain, and a sucking noise, as the butt pulled free of the earth. Gathering momentum, creating a great sigh as the air parted before it, the tree crashed down. Nearly 2200 years from the day when its first green shoot had poked up into the sunlight, it lay sprawled for its full 350 feet across the earth from which it had sprung.

And so the old monarch died. And yet it did not. For the roots that had severed when it had started its fall lay there beneath the ground, and within them still coursed the same flow of life. Early in the spring, up from these same roots, up into the life-giving light rose a dozen fresh shoots. These were not a new generation from seed: They were a continuation of the same tree life. They were the old tree itself, which had been metamorphosed into these new shapes. Through them it could live on and grow — *Sequoia sempervirens*, the ever-living.

MARTIN LITTON: *Redwood Creek forest*

JAMES ROSE: *Detail, forest floor, Prairie Creek*

2. REDWOODS THROUGH THE AGES

Sᴛᴀɴᴅɪɴɢ at the foot of a giant redwood, craning your neck to look up the soaring trunk, you sense your puniness. This tree, you are told, is probably well over a thousand years old. You are impressed, but you do not fully grasp the meaning of the figure until you reduce it to human terms, until you calculate that this tree was alive when William conquered England; that while forty, perhaps fifty generations of humans lived and loved and fought and died, this tree always stood in this very place, aloof and mindless of human antics.

No such convenient scale exists to help us comprehend the age of the redwoods as a race. Long before the first pre-humans lived, the redwoods were there. Before the first small mammal had evolved, the redwoods were there. Before the original primitive ancestors of most of today's plants had developed, the redwoods were there.

The first positively identified redwood fossils, represented by characteristic cones, date back to the Upper Jurassic period — some 130 million years ago. Could a man be transported back to those times, there would be little around him that he would recognize. The continents had not yet taken their present forms. The stresses in the earth's crust that would thrust up our great mountain chains, the Alps, the Himalayas, the Rockies, the Andes, had yet to build up.

A strange fauna then inhabited the earth. Swarms of sharks and ganoid fishes, huge marine reptiles — serpent-like plesiosaurs, dolphin-like ichthyosaurs — prowled the seas. Flying reptiles, which in the next period, the Cretaceous, would reach wingspreads of 15 to 20 feet, circled overhead. Dinosaurs of gigantic size and weird shapes were the lords of the land.

The flora was equally strange — great ferns, an enormous variety of cycads, and the many ancestors of that living fossil of today, the ginkgo or maidenhair tree. There were as yet no angiosperms, the flowering plants that dominate the vegetable kingdom today. But among all these bizarre and now long-vanished forms of life, the redwoods flourished.

Through 60 million years of the Cretaceous period, down into the Tertiary, they thrived and extended their sway, while the world's flora and fauna were being radically remade. Species after species of the dull-witted clumsy reptiles declined and became extinct. The age of mammals had begun. The little eohippus — the four-toed ancestor of the horse — primitive rhinoceroses, tapirs and camels, the forebears of the cat and dog tribes, inherited the earth. The plants, too, were changing. Broad-leafed conifers, juniper-like evergreen, then, later, hardwood trees such as the oaks and maples, hickory and ash we know today, displaced the earlier dominants.

By the Miocene, which began 25 million years ago, a redwood empire stretched across the northern hemisphere — from western Canada to the Atlantic, from France to Japan. In the United States, fossil remains of redwoods have been found in Texas, Pennsylvania, Colorado, Wyoming, Oregon, Washington, and California. In Yellowstone National Park, whole forests have been changed to stone by the mineral waters, or buried in showers of ashes from active volcanoes in the vicinity; sections of the trunks are 6 to 10 feet in diameter, and the butts still stand just as they grew, often 30 feet or more in height. In the petrified forest of Sonoma County are giant logs that were buried and turned to stone.

The Arctic was then no land of snow and ice but rather a humid and temperate region, and redwood fossils have been found in Spitzbergen, in Greenland, on many of the arctic islands north of the continent of North America, in Alaska and on St. Lawrence Island.

The redwoods in those times were as varied as they were far-flung. Paleobotanists have identified at least a dozen species. One, *Sequoia Reichenbachi,* found in Cretaceous clays, had cones almost like those of the Big Trees of the Sierra. The most common, *Sequoia Langsdorfi,* was almost indistinguishable from the modern *Sequoia sempervirens.* Still another, otherwise similar to the coast redwood, had the peculiarity that its twigs and cones had an opposite arrangement, whereas *Sequoia sempervirens* shows a spiral attachment of the twigs, needles and cone-scales; also its cones grew at the end of naked stalks instead of on needle-bearing twigs. To this fossil redwood was given the generic name *Metasequoia,* the dawn redwood, to distinguish it from the true Sequoias.

With the close of the Miocene, the redwoods began to retreat from the north. Over millions of years the climate grew colder and drier. The arctic became chill, then frozen, and where dense forests had stood, only lichens, dwarf willows, and sphagnum moss clothed the ground above the permafrost. Great icecaps formed, and in time the glaciers advanced to the south, inexorably bulldozing everything in their way. In Europe, where they had formed forests in England, France, Germany, Bohemia, Austria, Switzerland, the redwoods withdrew before the glaciers until they were back up against the Mediterranean — a Dunkirk in slow motion. Only there was no evacuation for them, no way by which they could escape across to Africa. And so they perished.

In Asia, land of the dawn redwood, the story was the same — or so it was thought until 1944. In that year, a forester chanced across an immense tree in a remote village of Szechuan province in central China. He had never seen one like it, so he brought out with him samples of twigs and cones. To their amazement, experts found them to be identical with *Metasequoia* fossil specimens gathered in Manchuria and Japan. Here, indeed, was a spectacular discovery: a fossil come to life, a tree thought dead for 25 million years but still growing, as it turned out, by the hundreds in an isolated region of Szechuan and neighboring

JAMES ROSE: *Snowfall, Bald Hills Road*

Hupeh provinces. In this one small area, where conditions of temperature and humidity were just right, this tree which once reigned from the Black Sea to Greenland had made its last stand.

In America, too, the redwood empire shrank. The southward march of the glaciers, great volcanic eruptions, and the upthrust of mountain ranges singly and collectively undid the work of 100 million years. In eastern Oregon, for instance, there had stood a mixed forest of dawn redwoods and of the immediate ancestors of our modern coast redwoods. Then the Cascades reared up their fiery summits in the path of the ocean winds. Today, eastern Oregon is an arid land, with rainfall sufficient only for the growth of scattered juniper trees and sagebrush.

As the redwoods' domain shrank, so did the number of their species. In time just two were left, and as it happened, California was where they both made their last bid for survival. The Big Tree, *Sequoia gigantea,* standing in isolated groves in the southern Sierra Nevada, and the redwood, *Sequoia sempervirens,* occupying a narrow strip along the northern California coast, are the last representatives of an heroic race, the last of the true sequoias, a living link to the age of dinosaurs.

JAMES ROSE: *Sand verbena, Gold Bluffs beach*

JAMES ROSE: *Sunset, Gold Bluffs beach*

The redwoods and the sea share primordial secrets.

Eons ago the sea knew the upthrust of mountains through its waters and the return of mountains to its depths. It helped to shape continents, and as age followed age, to consume them, and shape them again. Life first quickened within it and washed from it onto the warm shingles of the naked land.

No one knows when the first pliant shoot of redwood grew up from the primeval lands and a young tree pushed on triumphantly toward the sky. But 165,000,000 years ago the mud on a Manchurian plain locked inside itself a redwood frond.

Where did the redwoods come from? Was Asia, where that oldest redwood fossil lay so long, the cradle? Did the first forest flourish there and grow, and then begin an incredibly long, slow journey to the east and to the west, across the Arctic Circle to the far corners of the earth?

How did they travel there? Did they trust their seeds to the vagaries of the soft winds? Did they inch forward generation by generation across flatlands, up canyons and over mountains, taking a thousands years, the lifetime of a tree, to move a step?

— Peggy Wayburn

HOWARD KING: *Prairie Creek forest, along Ossagon Road*

Men have worked in many places. They have seen [life] creeping upward in the shape of lichens, among the howling winds of snow-clad mountains. They have seen it in the delicate "snowshoe" feet of desert lizards devised for running over sand. From some unknown spot, most probably along the shoals above the continental shelf, it has reached out into lakes and grasslands, edged stealthily into deserts, learned even to endure the heat of boiling springs or to hatch eggs, like the emperor penguin, in the blizzards by the southern pole. . . .

JAMES ROSE: *Saxifrage and spider, Middle Fork, Lost Man Creek*

It has similarly found its way into the downward cours-ing streams of the abyss. It has solved the pressures of the ocean bottom as it has survived the rarefied air of the high-est mountains. In these difficult surroundings life thins a little; the inventions that support it grow more difficult to produce and the intrusions are apt to be late, because life has experimented last in these bleak planetary wastelands.

Nevertheless the reaching out that began a billion years ago is still in process. The cells, so carefully transferring their limited range of endurance through astounding ex-tremes of heat and frost and pressure, show no inclination toward content. Content is a word unknown to life; it is also a word unknown to man.

— LOREN EISELEY, *The Immense Journey*

HOWARD KING: *Sitka spruce, Prairie Creek*

ANN ADAMS: *McArthur Creek forest*

3. TITANS OF THE COAST

B Y THEIR AGE, by their size, by their majestic beauty, the sequoias of California's coast and Sierra represent nature's supreme achievement in the evolution of trees. No other race of trees comes close to matching them. Nowhere else on earth are there groves or forests that compare with California's stands of sequoias.

Because of the sequoias' preëminence, because so many superlatives apply fittingly to both species, and because the two types live naturally in California and nowhere else (except a few coast redwoods in extreme southwestern Oregon), it is normal that some confusion between the two should have resulted in people's minds. Many probably assume that the coast and Sierra giants are the same tree, growing in two different localities. They are not. There is sufficient difference between them, in fact, for some botanists to have suggested that the Sierra Big Tree be given a different generic name, *Sequoiadendron giganteum* instead of *Sequoia gigantea,* reserving the name *Sequoia (sempervirens)* for its cousin of the coast.

Each of the two species has had its champions. John Muir, for one, was prejudiced in favor of the Sierra's Big Trees. Bret Harte went so far in his partisanship as to refer to the coast redwoods as the poor relations of the mountain species. In sheer craggy grandeur, in individual impressiveness, the Big Trees are without peer.

They are the biggest of all living things, and nearly the oldest — only the fantastic, gnarled bristlecone pine, whose wind-tortured shapes grow high in the White Mountains of California and other Great Basin ranges, is known to exceed the Big Tree's maximum lifespan of 4,000 years. In contrast, the greatest recorded age, by actual ring count, of a coast redwood is 2200 years. Though averaging 50 feet less in height than its coastal relatives — the tallest known giant sequoia, the California tree, measures 310 feet — it far surpasses them in girth and weight. Whereas mature coast redwoods average 12 to 16 feet in diameter, and none quite reaches 23 feet, hundreds of Big Trees are more than 25 feet through at the base, many reach 30 to 32 feet, and the General Grant, the world's thickest tree, has a base diameter of 40.3 feet and circumference of 107.6. The General Sherman tree, presumed to be the world's largest living thing, weighs an estimated 6167 tons; one of its limbs is larger than most of the trees in the Rocky Mountains.

On the other hand, "The Redwood, the ever-living Sequoia, *sempervirens,* is the tallest tree in the world," writes Donald Culross Peattie in *A Natural History of Western Trees.* "Not just occasionally taller, in individual specimens growing under unprecedently favorable conditions, but taller as a whole, as a race, a titan race." Yet as you walk among the redwoods, it is not so much the size of an individual tree that awes you. It is rather the impact of the forest as a whole, of the overwhelming ambiance of gigantism. For immensity is all about. There stands in Dyerville Flat a tree known as the Founders' Tree, dedicated to John C. Merriam, Henry Fairfield Osborn, and Madison Grant, founders of the Save-the-Redwoods League. This was long thought to be the tallest tree in the world until it was remeasured, and the title passed to a 359-foot giant in the Rockefeller Forest on Bull Creek Flat. This record was in turn surpassed by a tree of 367 feet discovered along Redwood Creek in 1964. But were it not for the signs pointing it out and the low fence about its base one would not single out the Founders' Tree for particular attention. It is only one titan in a legion of titans.

The tallest of trees is related closely to the greatest of oceans. From extreme southwestern Oregon to the Santa Lucia mountains below Carmel, the redwood forest extends for 450 miles in a narrow belt, averaging 20 miles in width. Sometimes growing almost to the Pacific shore, sometimes swinging inland for 30 or 40 miles as it follows the line of the coast ranges, the redwood never strays from the realm of the ocean winds.

At the south end of their range, in the Santa Lucias, the trees are confined to deep narrow canyons where streams and springs and shade compensate for the dry climate. Here the stand is thin, the trees scattered or isolated, and individual trees assume uncharacteristic shapes, with very long branches or irregular crowns or even flat tops.

Farther up the coast, in the Santa Cruz mountains, and, north of the Golden Gate Bridge, in the canyons of Marin and Sonoma and Mendocino counties, the redwoods grow more thickly, and there are many large, well-shaped trees. But it is mainly father north, in Humboldt and Del Norte counties, that the trees today reach their full stature, the forest its full glory. Here the winter rains are heaviest, ranging from 50 to 100 inches a year. And here the thickest fogs roll in on summer evenings to saturate the atmosphere and check evaporation from the leaves.

The relationship of climate and redwoods is reciprocal. So tall are the trees, so dense is the forest, that the redwoods themselves act as a climatic force. Were the forest not there to intercept and trap their moisture, the fogs would probably benefit neither plant, beast, nor man. There would be no rich undercover, no deep spongelike layer of decomposing leaves and needles to act as a reservoir, to keep the springs and creeks flowing in summer and to dam and regulate the overflow of water during winter storms. Without the anchoring power of the redwoods' great spreading roots and of the myriad tiny roots of plants that grow in their shade, the friable earth of the steep hillsides would wash into the gullies. Depending on the season, streams would be dry arroyos or raging, muddy torrents, and the salmon, steelhead, and trout would go elsewhere to spawn.

Much redwood country is rugged country. The coast giants do not adapt to high altitudes or snow; unlike the Big Trees of the Sierra, which grow at altitudes of 5,000 to 8,000 feet undisturbed by zero temperatures or deep snow drifts,

JAMES ROSE: *Detail, Douglas fir*

HOWARD KING: *Unnamed waterfall, Gold Bluffs beach*

the redwood never climbs above 3,000 feet. But if it boasts of no soaring peaks, this is still a sharply etched land, a land of high ridges and deep valleys. Its geological history makes its soils highly unstable, ever ready to seek a lower level, to be washed out to sea. It is a land of lovely, clear creeks, like Mill Creek, Blue Creek, Prairie Creek, and Redwood Creek, and, once upon a time, Bull Creek; bigger rivers such as the Russian River, the two Eels, and the Smith, coursing swift and strong in winter, or flowing serene between sand-and-gravel banks in summer's low-water months; and greatest of the lot, the deep, powerful Klamath.

It is finally an oceanic land both geographically and climatically. The tidal flux is never far away, and the influence of the sea is all-pervasive. The coast itself varies greatly in character. Along the Mendocino County shores, the combers boil and froth around the rocks and stacks offshore, or dash themselves against the rugged cliffline, deeply indented by narrow coves. Farther north the swells wash onto broad, straight beeches, piled high with driftwood. Behind the strands and dunes stretch peaceful lagoons, alive with the cries of waterfowl, or high bluffs with a dark crown of trees.

Throughout this region the redwood is king (or was before man altered much of the face of the land), but the aspect of the forest changes constantly — from slopes to flats, from streamside to seacoast. It changes also from south to north — as the climate becomes wetter, the undergrowth becomes lusher, more tangled and exuberant.

On the seaward edge of its belt, the redwood shares its domain with several magnificent species of conifers, such as the coast hemlock, the Sitka or tidelands spruce, the lowland fir and Lawson's cypress. On the slopes, at the heads of canyons or on the divides, the redwood admits the company of other trees — the Douglas fir, itself a noble tree which farther north, in Washington, attains a height of 325 feet; the aggresive tan oak; the madrone, with shiny green leaves and bright red satiny limbs. Shrubs grow thick in places — the California rosebay with its stunning rose-purple blooms; the fragrant western azalea; berry bushes like the California huckleberry, the thimbleberry with large velvety yellow-green leaves and downy bright red berries, the salmonberry with its luscious yellow fruit. Here and there a poison oak will climb a redwood trunk to heights of 50 to 150 feet, and to the human trespasser its autumnal riot of flaming leaves is aesthetic atonement for its toxicity.

The stream banks too have their own characteristic species. Here the bigleaf maple glows golden in the fall; the sunlight shimmers through thickets of red alders; mosses robe the tree trunks and beard their boughs; the five-finger fern hangs lovely fronds from the banks.

It is along the streams that wildlife, or the signs of its presence, can most often be seen. A black bear patrolling a sandy bank at dusk. A river beaver swimming downstream with a branch in its mouth, trailing a V-shaped wake. A great blue heron poised motionless at the water's edge, its sharp beak set to strike, or taking flight with a squawk, head tucked back and long legs trailing, and flapping its way to a roost high in a redwood's limbs. A startled mother merganser taking off low across the water, followed by her brood of ducklings frantically beating their stubby wings, not yet quite able to become airborne. A sharp-taloned osprey circling overhead on the alert for an unwary fish.

In the morning, the sand and mudbanks are like a hotel register, inscribed with the signatures of the visitors of the night: the delicate pointed hoofprints of deer, the great flat-footed, sharp-clawed tracks of bear, the small handlike prints of raccoon, occasionally the doglike tracks of a coyote or the rounded marks of a bobcat's soft pads.

Along the larger streams and rivers the redwoods form a solid curtain, shielding from prying eyes the mysteries of the forest. Here the great trees are limbed from crown to ground, and the protective screen of their foliage deflects the hurrying wind. Turn your back to the rippled stream, to the dancing light playing on the waters, part the leafy curtain, and you enter another world where time and space assume new dimensions.

It is on these riverside flats, often found at the confluence of two streams and built up gradually by the floods of the ages, that the redwood forest achieves a quintessence of majesty, an aura of holiness. There is something Olympian about the trees' massed ranks — if ever there were gods of trees, here they stand.

Away in all directions extend the vaulted naves. The ruddy pillars soar straight up, mighty beyond description, a mightiness that defies capture on printed page or photographic plate. Their buttressed bases seem to grip the earth with great leonine claws. Here and there a lumpy swelling mars the symmetry of a trunk. These huge burls, filled with dormant buds, sometimes resemble weird animals' heads, and you feel transported back to the dawn of time, watching a tyrannosaurus scratch its armored head against the bark.

The thick layer of needles and moss cushions your footsteps. The shamrock leaves and pretty pink-lavender blossoms of the redwood sorrel, oxalis, carpet the forest floor as far as the eye can see. The many ferns that grow luxuriantly from every hummock and every fallen trunk often attain great stature. The flowering plants for the most part hug the soil; their blossoms are usually small, inconspicuous, even minute. But they can bloom in such profusion that they change the whole atmosphere of the forest. Sometimes acres and acres are covered with the myriad tiny, pure white flowers of the sugar scoop, and then the aisles glow with a soft, strange light, as if the Milky Way had come to rest on the forest floor. Many of these little plants bear poetic names that strung together sound like a nosegay poor mad Ophelia might have picked: deer-foot, fringe-cup, inside-out flower, bleeding heart, milk-maid, fairy lantern, slim Solomon, fat Solomon, phantom orchis.

Time, time as we dissect it in days and hours and minutes, loses all meaning in a setting such as this. Here is a forest that was young when life itself was young. Here are trees that have already stood for a millenium or two — and still their lives will outlast yours a thousand years.

DONZEL WATSON: *Anemones, Prairie Creek*

ANN ADAMS: *Sand verbena and beach-bur, Gold Bluffs beach*

GORDON ROBINSON: *Hazel catkins, Mill Creek*

JAMES ROSE: *Forest pool on log, Prairie Creek*

HOWARD KING: *Forest detail, East Ridge Road, Prairie Creek*

JAMES ROSE: *Going . . . gone? Middle Fork, Lost Man Creek*

4. THE HAND OF MAN

ONE OF THE REDWOOD'S MYSTERIES is that it seems to have no natural lifespan. There is no biological reason known why one should ever die. The tannin that impregnates its bark and heartwood and gives them their rich red color makes the tree resistant to attacks of insects or fungi. The redwood normally is immune to ordinary tree diseases — accidental death is its usual fate. Despite the redwood's marvelous resistance to fire, fire can kill it, or so weaken it that a storm will overthrow it. Great winds will topple the more exposed trees. Ecological changes, too, can shorten a redwood's life — such as heavy compaction of the soil over its roots, or the interruption by one cause or another of the seepage of ground-water.

Over the ages, forces of climate and geology have reduced the redwoods to a small fraction of their former domain. It is possible that the same forces, of themselves, could in the end cause the total extinction of this ancient race — although they could just as well work to the redwoods' advantage and allow the trees to re-colonize lands once occupied by them.

Today, however, the redwoods face a more immediate threat than fire or tempest or frost or volcanic ash. Their greatest enemy, the most ruthless and methodical destroyer of the forests, is that animal which by its extraordinary abilities has become a geological force in its own right — modern man.

The first men to live among the redwoods had little effect on the forest. The Indians certainly started an occasional forest fire. Amazingly, they even did some logging, felling the giant trees without the use of a single metal tool. Using heated stones, they would burn a hole on one side of the tree, scraping off the charcoal with elkhorn tools until enough of the tree was cut away. Then a hole was made on the other side of the trunk, a little higher up. The Indians were skillful enough to be able to fell the tree in a given direction, and while one group made the cuts, another placed logs on the ground for a bed to receive the trunk as it fell. The same process of burn-and-scrape was used to buck the trunk into sections, after which boards were made by driving wedges of wood and elkhorn into the ends, splitting the logs into planks. These then were smoothed with stone adzes.

All this was naturally a slow, laborious process, and a redwood plank would become a treasured possession — even being handed down as an heirloom from one generation to the next. With such methods the Indians could do little to the forest as a whole. Lightning started more fires than they, and wind and rain claimed many times more trees.

Nor did the early white men have much impact on the redwoods. The Spaniards made light use of redwood, preferring to build in adobe. They did employ a few heavy beams in their churches and mission buildings, and history records that at his request Padre Junípero Serra, founder of California's chain of missions, was buried in 1784 in a redwood coffin at Mission San Carlos Borromeo in Carmel. Long lost in the church's ruins, the coffin was rediscovered 98 years after the burial, and found to be still in perfect condition.

The Russians, in pursuit of the sea otter, established in 1812 a colony at Fort Ross on the Mendocino coast and remained there until 1841, when the near-extinction of the otters and the failure of attempts at trade and agriculture decided the Russian-American Company of Alaska to sell its interest in the "Colony Ross" to Captain John Sutter of Sacramento. The Russians' buildings and stockade were made of redwood, and their chapel, built of hand-hewn redwood timbers, still stands to this day.

But it was not until the Gold Rush that the redwoods began to feel the hand of man. Even then, with timber for building purposes exceedingly scarce, redwood at first was regarded with contempt because of its softness, lightness and relative lack of strength. Houses were brought "around the horn" and set up in San Francisco and Oakland — one was even taken to Trinidad, in the very heart of the northern redwoods. Despite their original prejudice against it, the Forty-Niners made use of redwood because of its abundance and cheapness. And they soon found that it had more to commend it than price alone. "As timber the Redwood is too good to live," was John Muir's bitter comment. The wood has many of the same properties as the tree, and as a result the very qualities that protected the tree in the forest condemned it to destruction by man. Durable in contact with earth or water, rot- and termite-resistant, nonwarping, retentive of paint and easy to work, redwood was cut for everything from houses to wharf piles, from barns to sluice boxes, fences to water tanks, pipelines to shakes and shingles. And to top it all, the wood was almost as handsome as the tree. "As a wood for fine panelling it is a beauty," writes Peattie. "The heartwood needs no coloring but its own natural soft rich hue. More, it has an inexplicable golden gloss of its own, an halation as delicate as the shimmer on a tress of blond hair."

As early as 1850 sawmills were installed on the hills, south of San Francisco, which soon became a city of redwood houses. The stands of redwood on the Peninsula were heavily cut; in the East Bay hills, where their outline against the sky had been a landmark for ship captains entering the Golden Gate, the magnificent trees were logged off within a decade. In 1855 the first shipment by sea went from Humboldt County to San Francisco.

The redwoods were not cut only for their lumber. To many a hardy homesteader the great trees were but a nuisance, overgrown weeds to be cut or burned or rooted up. The laws of the time reflected the prevailing philosophy that the important thing was to get the land "settled up." And so, under the Pre-emption Law of 1841 and the Homestead Act of 1862 the bona fide settler could purchase 160 acres of redwood timberland at $1.25 an acre — no more than he would have had to pay for the same area of prairie grass or alkali flat.

The homesteader would proceed to clear his land as fast as possible. This was no task for the easily discouraged, for the redwood was not like the ordinary tree: not only was it a major project to cut one down, but also once felled the damned thing would not stay dead. The stump would at once send up a circle of hopeful shoots. In the virgin groves such circles of trees grown to giants can be seen standing around a charred stump more than a thousand years old. "All the brains, religion, and superstition of the neighborhood are brought into play to prevent a new growth," wrote John Muir. "The sprouts from the roots and stumps are cut off again and again, with zealous concern as to the best time and method of making death sure. In the clearings of one of the largest mills on the coast we found thirty men at work, last summer, cutting off redwood shoots 'in the dark of the moon,' claiming that all the stumps and roots cleared at this auspicious time would send up no more shoots."

But with time and enough perseverance, the homesteaders won out. Vineyards near the Russian River, sheep meadows on the Mendocino coast, cow pastures between Scotia and Eureka, on the lower Klamath and near Crescent City, are still sown with the burned-off stumps of hundreds of forest giants, some as large or larger than the biggest trees still standing along the Redwood Highway. "A sense of more than depression confronts the traveler who takes this desolation to heart," wrote John A. Crow in *California As a Place to Live.* "It is much the same impression left by the scorched earth found in the wake of a passing army.

"Eureka, which is beautifully situated, and could have been one of the most magnificent ports in the whole world, now lies in the midst of this destruction, a barren fishing and lumbering outpost in a denuded forest country. . . . [There] a few redwood trees shade the picnic grounds, but the countryside is an ugly wasteland of weeds and marshes. There is nothing here to remind the traveler of those immemorial groves which it took Nature so many centuries to create."

The same laws that were meant to benefit settlers proved a boon to timber speculators and operators, who were able to gain control fraudulently of vast tracts of public land under the commutation provision of the Homestead Act. With redwood timber averaging 90,000 board feet per acre and lumber selling for about $15 per thousand feet, one acre was grossing the mill about $1,350 for every $1.25 invested — a better than fair return on any investment. The greatest frauds were perpetrated under the Timber and Stone Act of 1878. In one notorious scheme at Eureka, farmers were stopped on their way home, merchants called from their counters and sailors lured from Coffee Jack's, a boarding house, and brought to the Land Office where land claims were filed for them. A shake shanty, often transportable, would be set up on a man's claim, to represent the homesteader's home. Then the homestead changed hands for a few dollars. The ultimate lumber operator often had to pay a fair price for his timber — but this profited nobody but the profiteer. Thus the government — and the American people — allowed the most valuable timber lands in the world to pass into the hands of a real or phony homesteader for a song.

But then these were the heroic days of lumbering, when the sheer brawn of men and beasts was pitted against the great trees. Swedes, Finns, and Norwegians, Frenchmen and Germans, Englishmen, Scotsmen and Irishmen, graduates of the Maine woods and "Bluenoses" from lower Canada made up the population of the redwood logging camps, and although they might have had trouble at times understanding each other they all shared the same pride in the depth and cleanness of their axe cuts.

The chopping boss, or bull buck, planned the strips to be cut, and a set of choppers might work from a month to three months on one strip. A staging was built around the trunk of a tree above the butt swell and on this the pair of choppers stood. Their equipment included two axes, two eight-foot saws, one twelve-foot saw, two dozen plates, one dozen shims, ten wedges, two sledges, one pair of gun stocks, one plumb bob. This last item was all-important, for with it the choppers determined whether the tree was straight or a leaner, and if the latter they adjusted their cut so as to make it fall in the right direction (usually uphill), where a bedding of smaller trees and branches had been prepared to fill in the low spots and to cushion its fall. It was bad luck to the crew that made the slightest miscalculation, for they could bring hundreds of tons of wood crashing down on their heads. Or the tree could fall afoul of its layout and shatter into fragments; hundreds of dollars' worth of wood would be abandoned on the ground and the loggers would move on to the next tree, all their sweat and toil having gone for naught. Felling a giant redwood up to 12 feet in diameter with hand axe and crosscut saw often took as much as three days.

Once felled, the trunk was cut into lengths suitable to the market, and the barkers pried off the bark with long poles. Then it was up to the jackscrewers to roll the logs within reach of the bull team crew — a dangerous job as the log would sometimes take an unexpected roll. Teams of bulls or oxen (or sometimes horses) hauled the logs down the skid road to the riverside dump. A string of logs was joined by chains and dog-hooks, with the heaviest butt, weighing up to 20 tons, in the lead. On this the chain-tender rode, keeping a sharp eye on the water-carrier, often a Chinese, whose duty it was to go between the head log and the rear oxen and wet the skids in the road so the logs would slide more easily. "The six to eight yoke of bulls tugging at the long line of bumping logs is one of the most animated scenes in a lumber camp," an eyewitness wrote. "These brutes are of enormous size, stolidly obedient to the 'Whoa haws' and 'Gees' of the teamsters, and surprisingly quick to get out of the way of a flying log. In a hard pull the faithful creatures fairly get down upon their knees to make it."

At the dump, or landing, the jackscrewers took over once more, rolling the logs into the river. (Another common method of bringing the logs to the river was to send them in a box flume — an exciting sight as each naked bole came smoking down at terrific speed, making a huge splash as it struck the water.) Once in the river the logs remained on the spot until the rainy season when freshets could move them. When the rains came, whether it was midnight or daytime, the log drivers were routed out to rush the log jam down the swollen river. Sluice dams were sometimes built to gather a head of water. When enough water had backed up behind the dams they were "tripped" or broken, and the logs were shot down to the mill in the ensuing flash flood.

This system of floating the logs down streams lasted in Humboldt County until about 1880, when logging railroads generally superseded it. In Mendocino County the log drives lasted much longer. In 1928, 20 million board feet of redwood were successfully flushed down Big River, and the last dam was tripped as late as 1936. The Mendocino streambanks still show the scouring effect of the log drives. It was in Mendocino, too, that the most picturesque methods were used to ship out the lumber. The rugged coast has few natural harbors, but the lumber schooners worked their way into the small coves or dog holes, mooring under the high sheer cliffs with the aid of their own anchors or of a makeshift buoy. An apron chute extended from the top of the cliff to the ship's pitching deck, and down this the lumber slid. Or it was lowered on swaying slings suspended from a wire cable, one end of which was anchored to the cliff and the other in the cove or ocean. Sometimes whole logs weighing many tons were swung aboard by this method.

At about the time when steam locomotives, dragging long strings of log-carrying flatcars across vertiginous trestles, became a common sight in the redwood region, another type of steam engine could be heard chugging in the woods. "In 1881," writes Peattie, "John Dolbeer, a pioneer operator among the Eureka redwoods, brought out of his blacksmith shop an invention that made the bullwhackers guffaw. It was a sort of donkey engine with a vertical boiler, a horizontal one-cylinder engine, and a big drum on which to wind up the tentacles of steel cable. He made these fast to a gigantic log, then opened up his engine wide. The log came thrashing down the skid road faster than the bullwhackers could cuss an ox, and the smirks died from their faces, for their jobs were gone."

The transition was actually not quite that sudden — the last straining bull team was used in 1914 — but the "Dolbeer Donkey" and its more powerful offspring quickly revolutionized logging. More efficient than the slow, plodding oxen, they were also far more destructive. The hauling of logs no longer was confined to skid roads; the butts came crashing through the forest from every direction, ploughing up the ground, crushing the undergrowth, bulldozing young trees in their path. Even more devastating were the fires set by the loggers. "This Big Basin country is an example, and I can speak on this matter from personal observation," wrote a resident of the Santa Cruz mountains in 1900. "How often, in the hottest of the summer, have I not wished bad luck to the suffocating smoke that covers our beautiful scenery as with a black pall, day after day, hiding the face of Ben Lomond with an unsightly veil, and increasing the temperature by at least ten degrees. If you ask, 'Where is the fire? — it must be doing a great deal of damage,' the aborigine of the mountains will answer with the utmost indifference, 'Oh, no; they are only burning brush in the Big Basin.' Sounds quite harmless, does it not?

"But the burning away of the underbrush means this: a certain section has been designated, or rather doomed, by the owner, to be cleared; that is, the big trees (redwoods) are to be felled and made ready for the sawmill. When the mighty monarchs of the forest lie prone at last, the entire bark is stripped from off their trunk. . . . Then the torch is applied some fine dark night, and everything in that section, the birds in their nests, the merry little tree-squirrel, the swift deer and the spotted fawn, the giant ferns and the rare orchids — everything is burned to death. The enormous trunks of the redwoods, green and full of sap, alone resist the fire-fiend; tops, branches, bark, are all burned to ashes, and madroños, oaks, firs, and young redwood trees are reduced to cinders and pitiful-looking black stumps."

Such protests were of little avail against an industry that by the turn of the century had become the most important in the state. As the population grew so did its demand for wood — in all of its uses. And such was the versatility of redwood that its applications were practically unlimited. Dr. W. L. Jepson gave a striking summary of them in his *The Silva of California* (1923): "The writer of these lines is a Californian. He was rocked by a pioneer mother in a cradle made of Redwood. The house in which he lived was largely made of Redwood. His clothing, the books of his juvenile library, the saddle for his riding pony were brought in railway cars chiefly made of Redwood, running on rails laid on Redwood ties, their course controlled by wires strung on Redwood poles. He went to school in a Redwood schoolhouse, sat at a desk made of Redwood and wore shoes the leather of which was tanned in Redwood vats. Everywhere he touched Redwood. Boxes, bins, bats, barns, bridges, bungalows were made of Redwood. Posts, porches, piles, pails, pencils, pillars, paving-blocks, pipe lines . . . were made of Redwood. . . .

"One of the most emphatic tributes to the economic value of Redwood is that new uses are constantly being discovered for it. We ship our choicest grapes to distant lands packed in Redwood sawdust. We replace steel water-conduits with Redwood. We supply Redwood doors to the Central American market because the white ant does not eat Redwood."

And so, being too good to live, the redwoods continued to fall by the thousands every year. The 20th Century brought increasing mechanization to logging operations. Both in the woods and the mills methods became more and more efficient and less backbreaking to the men. The gasoline-powered chainsaw replaced the old handsaws, and lopped off the trees like a guillotine. In 1935, crawler tractors began to drag the logs to the landings, rendering the donkey engine obsolete. Except where the ground is too steep and high-lead logging — cable-hauling the logs up abrupt slopes — is necessary, the cats are used almost exclusively today. Huge off-highway trucks generally supplanted the logging railroads

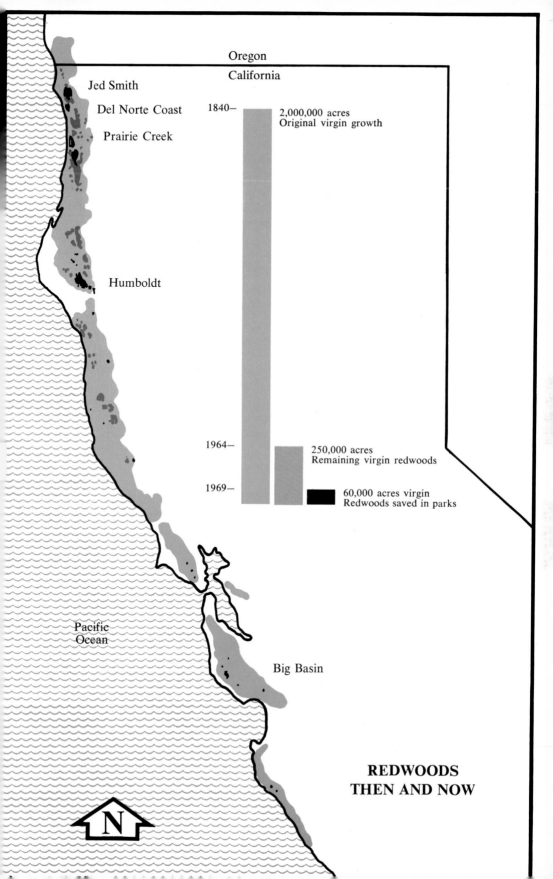

Oregon

California

Jed Smith

Del Norte Coast

Prairie Creek

Humboldt

1840 —

2,000,000 acres
Original virgin growth

1964 —

250,000 acres
Remaining virgin redwoods

1969 —

60,000 acres virgin
Redwoods saved in parks

Pacific
Ocean

Big Basin

**REDWOODS
THEN AND NOW**

N

in the task of bringing the logs from landing to mill, and dusty logging roads everywhere penetrated the forest, making accessible even the most remote stands.

For the first 30 years of the century, the annual cut averaged 500,000,000 board feet of redwood. During the depression years of the 'thirties this dropped to 300,000,000. But in World War II the drain on the forests accelerated. Immense quantities of redwood timber were rushed to the Pacific theater. Wartime restrictions on home construction and other consumer uses of wood limited the cut. But the demand was there, accumulating like water behind a dam. And with V-J Day the dam burst. The tempo of cutting speeded up and by the early 'fifties reached 1 billion board feet of redwood a year. The number of sawmills in the redwood region (including those sawing Douglas fir and other species) jumped from 117 in 1945 to 299 in 1947 and 398 in 1948. Most of the new mills were small outfits that would log a plot of land and then close down — throughout the redwood belt one runs across the rusting ruins of such fly-by-night mills. Too many of them operated on the cut and get out principle — interested only in making a quick profit, the owners cared not how they treated the land, and left it in no condition to reforest itself. Many specialized in so-called split products — chopping up thousand-year-old trees into grapestakes and fencing and shingles.

Today, the snarling whine of the chainsaws, the growl of huge cats everywhere rend the silence of the woods. Herds of gigantic trucks come thundering down from the hills in clouds of dust, dwarfed by the logs they carry, and jam up the tourist traffic along the Redwood Highway. In the big mills' yards can be seen whole forests of trees — massive decks of logs each thicker than a man is tall, rows of towering stacks of rough-cut lumber. Back in the woods the logged-off sections look like Tarawa after the Marines had landed. Where once a carpet of redwood sorrel and lady fern spread there is nothing but bare earth, churned up by the tractors' treads and strewn with slash — tree tops, branches, shattered pieces of trunks and sundry other logging waste. Muddy streams, with beds obstructed by debris, run between denuded banks, sorry reminders of the beautiful clear creeks that once cheered the forest with their music. Great stumps rise from the ground like the tombstones of trees. And the redwoods left standing to reseed the forest look like caricatures. They soon clothe their nude flanks from butt to crown with fuzzy foliage, almost as if ashamed of their sudden exposure. Seen from the air, logged areas are an intricate maze of tractor trails, like worm tracks under the bark of an infested tree, and the boundaries of state parks are as sharply defined as on a map.

The biggest, most beautiful, and accessible trees are going first. How much longer can this destruction last? Not very long. In 1909, there were an estimated 102 billion board feet of old-growth redwood in the forests; in 1920, 72 billion; in 1931, 57 billion. By 1953, the U.S. Forest Service estimated that the "live sawtimber volume" of redwood, including some second growth, was down to 35 billion board feet. And in 1960 the Forest Service predicted that at the current rate of cutting the bulk of virgin redwood in private hands (and 93 per cent of the old growth is in private hands) would be gone by 1980. The increasing commercial use of redwood and the expanding population are likely to shorten this estimate. All the inventive talents of the industry, all the promotional talents of the California Redwood Association, are devoted to increasing the use and uses of redwood, to spurring domestic demand for redwood products and finding new markets abroad. Taxes on standing timber are levied by counties in the redwood belt regardless of whether the owner is in the timber business. It matters not to the tax assessor whether the owner wants to log or not: the trees must be converted into dollars. And in fact the taxes have been greater for the owner not in the timber business. And many an owner of small timber lands — a rancher, for instance, or the proprietor of a resort — who may want to keep his trees finds that he cannot afford to do so, and so he sells his timber to the loggers. Emanuel Fritz, professor emeritus of forestry at the University of California and consulting forester to the California Redwood Association, wrote in April 1963 to the Save-the-Redwoods League: "I used to think that these groves are safe in the hands of the owners who, for some time, were apparently doing well running resorts for tourists and campers. But this is all changed. High taxes, and increased costs of running a 90-day tourist camp make it impossible to own old-growth redwoods as an attraction when their competitors have no such expense. As to the taxes, you have here an excellent example of the power of taxation to destroy."

With every proud owner of a new redwood home, with every suburbanite who repanels his living room with redwood or beautifies his patio with redwood planters and furniture, the end of the great trees draws nearer. It takes a redwood 400 years or more to mature. Man, armed with chainsaw, can cut it down in an hour. It took nature over 100 million years to create the world's most sublime forest. Within a few years the remnants of the virgin forest will be gone — destroyed by man in little more than a century.

JAMES ROSE: *Before: Middle Fork, Lost Man Creek, November, 1967*

JAMES ROSE: *After: same place, May, 1968*

Visitors to the area sometimes express concern over appearance of the land immediately after logging. . . . It takes big equipment to move the heavy logs over steep country. The ground does get scuffed. Like a corn field just after harvest, it presents a ruffled picture.
— ARCATA REDWOOD COMPANY FOLDER

GORDON ROBINSON: *Logging exhibit, road to Gold Bluffs beach*

5. CONSERVATION OR PRESERVATION?

"I FEEL MOST EMPHATICALLY that we should not turn into shingles a tree which was old when the first Egyptian conqueror penetrated to the valley of the Euphrates, which it has taken so many thousands of years to build up, and which can be put to better use. That you may say is not looking at the matter from the practical standpoint. There is nothing more practical in the end than the preservation of beauty, than the preservation of anything that appeals to the higher emotions in mankind."

In this speech, made 60 years ago, Theodore Roosevelt was talking about the Sierra Big Trees. But he could have said much the same of the coast redwoods — except that the oldest of these may date its birth only at a century or two before Christ. And yet, of perhaps 2,000,000 acres of redwoods whose majestic ranks covered northern California's coastal hills and valleys before logging began, only 107,279 acres — and not all of virgin growth (only 50,000 acres is virgin) — have been set apart in the state parks to "appeal to the higher emotions in mankind." The balance has been dedicated for over a century to the manufacture of shingles and other products of the lumber industry.

And despite the rapidly dwindling reserves of old-growth timber, the liquidation of these reserves continues at an accelerated pace, as if the forests were inexhaustible. The forests are indeed inexhaustible, if properly managed, the argument runs. One would think the major lumber companies in the area, who own or have cutting rights on a large proportion of redwood timberlands, would have a vested interest in staying in business and would increasingly try to log in such a fashion that their lands would be left in a productive condition — if their goal is sustained or perpetual yield. The realization that conservation makes economic sense has widened to the point where an increasing number of operators and owners of timberlands are trying to manage their holdings so that their first crop of redwood will not be their last.

It took a long time for such an attitude to develop, for loggers to realize — or care — that unless nature were treated with respect it would rebel and refuse to grow anything but brush where redwoods once had thrived. The donkey engine and cable-yarding method used from 1881 to the 1930s was so destructive that it left cut-over lands almost devoid of a seed source. But it was not until 1923 that a systematic program of planting was undertaken. Large nurseries were established and the nursery seedlings were planted by hand on the cut-over lands.

But seedling mortality was high, especially during the hot summer months. The depression brought this attempt to an abrupt end.

In the mid-'thirties two related innovations seemed to give the redwood forest a new lease on life. One was the advent of the crawler tractor, which soon made the donkey engine and wire-cable logging obsolete. Self-propelled and maneuverable, the tractor could in theory skirt young trees and thus avert the wholesale destruction of all plant life that cable logging entailed. At the same time, the selective logging principle was first applied to the redwoods — a principle which in Montana was humorously defined as "You select a mountain and you log it." But as described by the lumber companies the selective logging theory seems to make sense. A virgin stand of redwoods is made up of trees of all ages — just as the population of a city includes babies and octogenarians. The older trees — the veterans of a thousand years or more — grow very slowly, and by usurping sunlight and moisture and the nutrients in the soil they slow the growth of the younger trees. From the point of view of a logger, who appraises a forest in board feet, such a stand is static or overmature. Nature, working by her own methods, has practiced forest renewal so successfully that our present redwoods are the direct, recognizable descendants of trees that thrived in the age of dinosaurs. It has created such marvels as the Rockefeller Forest in Bull Creek Flat. But in a way, it has botched the job: from the practical standpoint it would be better to clear out the old trees and give the younger ones a chance to come into their own. For a young redwood, once released by natural causes or by logging from the tyranny of its elders, is one of the fastest growing of trees.

This rapid early growth, and the peculiar ability of a redwood once cut to resprout from stump or roots, form the basis of the selective cutting rationale. Step one is to cut down the old giants, leaving the younger trees to grow more rapidly in volume and quantity, to provide seed for natural regeneration, to shade the ground against too-rapid desiccation during the dry summers and to protect the soil against erosion. From the stumps of the old trees new sprouts will shoot up. Step two, some years later, is to log off the release growth of younger trees which by then will have attained merchantable proportions. The seedlings which these will have sowed and the stump sprouts from the original growth will be harvested at step three of the cycle. And so on in perpetuity.

Guard against fire, except for controlled burning of slash, take a few precautions to minimize soil erosion, leave a few trees standing to provide seed for regeneration, and in theory the redwoods can be harvested periodically like any other crop, like alfalfa or cotton or black-eyed peas. "Visitors to the area sometimes express concern over appearance of the land immediately after logging," a major redwood logging company's brochure concedes. "It takes big equipment to move the heavy logs over steep country. The ground does get scuffed. Like a cornfield just after the harvest, it presents a ruffled picture. But people are not alarmed at the appearance of a cornfield because they know that next year a new crop will stand in its place. We call our forest lands TREE FARMS, but we plan to take many years between harvests. When the time has passed, the land will be full again, just like the cornfield will be next year."

In 1950, 16 years after the introduction of selective cutting to the redwood region, the first redwood tree farm was certified. Since then 600,000 acres of redwood timberlands have been designated as tree farms. In a way, the certification of a tree farm is like the ordination of a priest or the admittance of a lawyer to the bar: It is the industry itself which, through the California Redwood Association, decides what standards of forestry are required on a tree farm and whether an individual operation meets these standards or not. The basic principles for eligibility to become a tree farmer are: (1) To assure the California Redwood Association of willingness to maintain the land designated as a tree farm in a condition to produce forest crops under good forest practices; (2) To provide reasonable protection from fire and other damage, including excessive grazing; (3)To harvest the crop of standing timber on the tree farm in a manner which will assure further crops; (4) To furnish information concerning his tree farm when requested to do so by the California Redwood Association, such information to embrace progress, future plans, improvements, protection, and cutting practices. But whereas an errant priest can be defrocked or a lawyer disbarred, a logger who fails to observe minimum sound logging practices cannot be prevented from operating by his peers. The tree farm movement is self-policing, but the policeman has no weapon but scorn. Although certification as a "Tree Farm" implies an even, sustained flow of forest crops, but does not require it. And annual cut still substantially exceeds annual growth.

Yet self-regulation by the industry is the only practical form of regulation in effect at present. The Forest Practice Act, passed by the California Legislature in 1946 and since amended, has the stated purpose "to conserve and maintain the productivity of the timberlands in the interest of the economic welfare of the state and the continuance of the forest industry; to establish . . . standards of forest practice . . . adopted to promote the maximum sustained productivity of the forest. . . ." Pursuant to the act, rules were established requiring certain minimum measures for "fire prevention and control, for protection against timber operations which unnecessarily destroy young timber growth or timber productivity of the soil, for prevention and control of damage by forest insects, pests and disease, and measures for the restocking of the land." The act requires timber owners to file notices of intended operations with the State Forester and loggers in order to obtain yearly operating permits. It also specifies penalties for violations of the Forest Practice Rules developed by individual Forest Practice Committees in four different Forest Practice Districts throughout the state.

How effective has the Forest Practice Act been? Not very. A comprehensive study of ways of reforming the act, carried out by Phillip S. Berry, of the Sierra Club's legal committee, revealed major shortcomings. As far as erosion control is concerned, the act has provided no comprehensive standards or guidelines for judging whether there has been compliance with the law. The word "erosion" is not used at all in the language of the act itself. Presumably, the individual rule-making committees were left to figure out for themselves what forces cause erosion. As a result, the committees have foundered. One set of rules enjoins the operator to "take all reasonable steps . . . to maintain the productivity of timberlands in his logging area and . . . [to exercise] due diligence . . . to prevent . . . washout or gullying. . . ." But what are all reasonable steps? What is due diligence? Would a Vehicle Code that merely admonished drivers to be careful and to exercise due diligence be adequate? Until 1967 the logging rules applied in the Redwood Region were a virtually meaningless hodgepodge which did not deal at all with the most important erosion producing activities of loggers. Largely as a result of legal action taken by the Sierra Club, the redwood logging rules were then amended to include within their scope all the major causes of erosion connected with logging. Unfortunately, the language of the rules is still very general and the vagueness that results makes enforcement more difficult.

If the rules are inadequate, the enforcement provisions are even more so. The Legislature up to now has budgeted for only eight regular inspectors to canvass the entire state. The efforts of these men are supplemented by the work of other part-time personnel, bringing the total inspection force to approximately sixteen. The typical timber operator has several operations going at once and these average 115 acres in size. On the average, an operator is inspected slightly more than once per year. Thus, the ordinary operation is inspected less than once a year. That single inspection lasts about two hours and includes perhaps fifteen minutes on the subject of erosion control. To say the least, at present, only token efforts are being made to enforce the existing law designed to prevent erosion, and photographs in this book show the grim result.

The enforcement provided is equivalent to cutting down the Highway Patrol to the point where a driver would see a patrolman on the highway only once a year. The Legislature does not have such faith in the capacity of the average motorist for self-regulation, and has good reason to have less faith in the standards of the average logger.

Finally, the act contains a major loophole. Upon the simple affidavit of the timberland owner stating a bona fide intention to put the land to other use, the owner may chop down every tree on his property regardless of the suitability of his land for the substituted use, or the erosion that results. Not only has erosion often ruined the land converted, but it has also frequently damaged adjoining property and property lower on the same watershed. And according to a 1956 report of the Division of Forestry, "There is some feeling that people who do not wish to observe the Forest Practices Rules have found it convenient to utilize certain exemptions provided [by this loophole] to escape compliance with the rules without carrying out the intent of devoting the land to other than timber-growing use."

The effectiveness of the existing law controlling erosion and its enforcement can be judged by measuring the erosion itself. Data compiled by the U.S. Department of Interior show the current annual soil loss from some North Coast drainages to be extremely high. Some watersheds have lost five to six pounds of soil per square yard per year. In 1963, the year before the big flood, twenty-two million tons of suspended sediment were carried into the Pacific by the Eel River alone. The average rate of erosion over most of the North Coast area where the redwoods live has been calculated to be approximately fifty times the natural rate. While logging is not the sole cause of this accelerated erosion, it is the prime cause. Aside from the construction of highways, timbering operations are the only activities of man in the affected watersheds. Consequently, it does the loggers little good to point fingers at others.

Obviously, our redwood logging companies are going to have to exhibit greater care and respect for their lands if these are not in time to become barren wastes incapable of supporting redwoods or anything else. Standards will need to be a good deal higher and enforcement much stricter if tree farming and sustained yield are to be more than public relations slogans. And one begins to be somewhat skeptical of such statements as that once made by Professor Fritz, that "the future of the redwood forests has never been more secure." To be sure, there are areas that were logged long ago where there are now fine stands of second-growth redwood. In other areas, however, the quality of the second-growth redwood has proved so disappointing that owners have turned to clear cutting the redwood, bulldozing the land, and reseeding with Douglas fir. Immediately south of Prairie Creek Redwoods State Park, Highway 101 traverses a scene of apocalyptic devastation, where not a tree was left standing. But big signs along the road try to reassure the passing public: "14,000,000 seeds planted on 200 tree farm acres," they read. And at a roadside pavilion the traveler can view samples of redwood siding and paneling, and can pick up pamphlets titled "Forest Renewal Story." What neither signs nor pamphlets mention is that the company has reseeded not with redwood but with Douglas fir, spruce, and cedar. [The most prominent sign of all is now gone, as are, apparently, most of the hoped-for seedlings. — Ed.]

It would be unfair at this time, only 13 years after the first tree farm was certified in the redwood region, to dismiss the goal of perpetual yield as a mirage, or to conclude that tree farms are just a public relations device. But by the same token one may validly question whether a few decades' experience with sustained yield practices is sufficient to justify industry predictions that once the virgin redwood stands are liquidated the lumber interests "will have continuing supplies of [second growth] forests for maintaining a steady flow of products to the homebuilders and industries." Indeed, one may legitimately wonder whether redwoods can really be harvested like any other crop, whether tree farm is an apt term for a logging operation, no matter how scientific.

Under natural conditions, a redwood forest may take from 400 to 1,000 years to replace itself. Yet the companies plan to shorten the renewal cycle to 50 years or so. In a virgin forest, the total mass of organic matter — of living trees and other plants, of decomposing wood and foliage — remains more or less constant, in a continuous cycle of life and growth and death and decay. But when loggers harvest the forest and remove the wood they have cut, there is a net loss to the forest of organic matter. In real farming, farmers compensate for this loss by fertilizing their fields. Tree farmers do nothing of the kind. It might be more accurate to describe their operations as tree mining, since in a very real sense loggers mine the organic wealth of the forests. They have a boundless faith in Nature's ability to heal its wounds — and to continue doing so every half century. But does a second growth not represent a stretching of the membrane of life? Will a third growth and fourth growth and fifth growth stretch the membrane increasingly thin — to the point where eventually it must tear? Is there no danger that the periodic mining of the forest's organic wealth and the repeated disturbance of its soil (with the resulting erosion) will in the end lead to the total exhaustion of the land?

At our present level of knowledge such questions have no answers. "We know next to nothing about forest soils," admitted Bernard Frank when he was assistant chief of the U.S. Forest Service. The bulk of the redwood being cut is still virgin growth, and not until several forest generations have been grown and logged, not until fifth- and sixth-growth trees are being sawed at the mills will we know if sustained yield can really be sustained. If we were really as scientific as we pretend to be and really cared about the perpetuation of our redwoods, we should probably halt all logging except on experimental stands, where different methods of clear or selective cutting could be tried and evaluated over a number of logging and growing cycles. Only then, if the results justified it, would large-scale logging be resumed, just as a new surgical technique wins general adoption only after it has been thoroughly tested first on laboratory animals and then on hopeless human subjects. But the public demands redwood products, the industry has a big investment in plants and equipment, the counties of the redwood region depend largely on timber taxes — and so the public will continue to buy redwood homes, the industry to reap its profits, and the counties to collect their taxes even at the risk of ultimate deforestation — the very process which turned the Middle East, once a land of milk and honey, into a barren and desert land.

The most we can hope for is that conservation measures practiced by the best in the industry will be adopted by all, that continued refinements in the mills will further reduce wastage — a saving at the mills that means a saving of trees — and that nature will play along with the loggers by growing as much redwood as they can cut. But conservation is a word that has two meanings in the redwood area. One is economic conservation — the kind with which the lumber companies are concerned. The other is esthetic. It is the kind of conservation that seeks to preserve the virgin redwoods in their natural state, as the world's finest forest, as a unique treasure which once lost can never be regained. Preserving the redwoods has nothing to do with the success or failure of the sustained-yield experiment. For no matter how vigorous, a second-growth redwood forest aesthetically is a second-rate redwood forest. There is nothing inspirational about a stand of

EDGAR WAYBURN: *Overlooking Big Lagoon, logged in the late fifties*

slim young redwoods with an arbitrarily set life expectancy of 50 years or so. There is nothing unique about them, either. They have a beauty of their own, to be sure — but so do young evergreens everywhere. They will never match the majesty, the mystery, the primeval beauty of the virgin redwoods, for they will not be given the chance to do so. If these qualities are worth preserving for themselves, if, as Theodore Roosevelt said, "There is nothing more practical in the end than the preservation of beauty," then the highest form of conservation is the maintenance in their natural state of as many of our virgin redwoods as possible.

JAMES ROSE: *Before: Middle Fork, Lost Man Creek, April, 1968*

JAMES ROSE: *After: same place, June, 1968. Stump 13 feet in diameter, 1,040 rings*

. . . this temple which the Great Architect has been building for a score of centuries is incomparably nobler, more beautiful and more serene than any erected by the hands of man. Its nave is loftier than that of Amiens and longer than that of St. Peter's. Its wine-red shafts, rising clean and straight over two hundred feet, are more numerous than the pillars of Cordova;

MARTIN LITTON: *North Fork, Lost Man Creek. Foreground selectively logged; middle
ground clean logged*

MARTIN LITTON: *Clean logging, North Fork, Lost Man Creek. Standing trees approximately 300 feet tall*

DAVID VAN de MARK: *Clean logging, headwaters of Elam and McArthur creeks*

its floor is carpeted with a green and brown mosaic
more intricate than that of St. Mark's;

JAMES ROSE: *Clean logging, North Fork, Lost Man Creek*

its aisles are lit with a translucence more beautiful than that which filters through the stained glass of Chartres; its spires pierce higher than those of Cologne; its years are greater than those of the first lowly building devoted to Christian service.

— DUNCAN MCDUFFIE

JAMES ROSE: *After the show is over . . . North Fork, Lost Man Creek*

MARTIN LITTON: *Meadow and primeval forest, lower Redwood Creek*

6. "SAVING" THE REDWOODS

"ANY FOOL CAN DESTROY TREES," John Muir once wrote. "They cannot run away; and if they could they would still be destroyed — chased and hunted down as long as fun or a dollar could be got out of their bark hides, branching horns, or magnificent bole backbones. . . . God has cared for these [Sequoias], saved them from drought, disease, avalanche, and a thousand straining, leveling tempests and floods; but He cannot save them from fools — only Uncle Sam can do that."

Spurred on by conservationists, Uncle Sam early came to the rescue of the Sierra Big Trees. Yosemite, ceded to California in 1864 to be a park for all the nation, became a national park per se in 1890. In that same year Sequoia National Park and the General Grant Grove were preserved by federal acts. Today, close to 97 per cent of the virgin stand of *Sequoia gigantea* is protected in national parks, national forests, or state parks. Outside these reserves there is still sporadic cutting of these magnificent trees, despite their unsuitability as timber, and operators try to pass off the lumber as redwood.

But Uncle Sam took no such interest in the coast redwoods. In 1900 not one of these trees enjoyed public protection; on every redwood alive the logging season was permanently open. Luckily there were men and women who found this scandalous, and in May 1900 they formed the Sempervirens Club of California and began to campaign for the establishment of a public park in the coastal redwoods. They did their work well: prominent citizens throughout the state rallied to the cause, as did important scientific bodies in the eastern states and other localities outside California, and in 1902 the legislature approved a bill appropriating $250,000 for the purchase of 3800 acres of redwoods in Big Basin, in the Santa Cruz mountains. Five years later, Congressman William Kent snapped up 295 acres of redwoods sheltered in a canyon at the southwest base of Mount Tamalpais just ahead of a water company that wanted to flood the canyon. And the next year Kent gave his purchase to the people of the United States in honor of his friend John Muir, and President Theodore Roosevelt accepted it under authority of the Antiquities Act. Today Muir Woods National Monument, expanded to 510 acres by a further gift from Kent, is the most visited redwood grove, standing as it does less than an hour's drive north of San Francisco.

These two groves, another protected by Santa Cruz County, a small tract owned by Sonoma County and another by the Bohemian Club, were the only redwoods protected against the loggers' saws when the United States entered

World War I. At that time, a new threat developed to the northern redwoods. The State decided to rebuild the highway running north from San Francisco to the Oregon border. The new road would give lumbermen easier access to the finest stands of all, and it seemed a fair bet that the Humboldt and Del Norte redwoods would shortly be falling like grain before the scythe. In the summer of 1917 three prominent conservationists — Henry Fairfield Osborn, president of the American Museum of Natural History; John C. Merriam, then professor of paleontology at the University of California and afterward for 18 years president of the Carnegie Institution of Washington; and Madison Grant, an amateur scientist and president of the New York Zoological Society — took a sightseeing trip through the Humboldt redwoods. And what they saw appalled them. As Dr. Osborn described it, "There are parts of the northwestern highways where for miles the road is narrowed and blocked with piled grape stakes and shingles, and on either hand the ground is covered with a jumble of treetops, branches, slabs, and bark, which should have gone into the manufacture of some by-product.

"But," he added, "also there are stretches where the roadway leads from open sunshine and distant views of green, wooded mountain slopes into the giant forest and on through colonnades of trees where the air is cool and fragrant and long beams of sunlight slant down through the green of redwood foliage." The three men returned from the northern woods determined that some, at least, of the colonnades would remain vertical. And they wasted no time in setting up an organization and a plan of action. Early in 1918 they founded the Save-the-Redwoods League, which at once began to collect members and funds — and publicity for its cause. Articles by Osborn and Grant in the *National Geographic* and by Albert Atwood, Joseph Hergesheimer, and Samuel G. Blythe in the *Saturday Evening Post* began to awaken the American public to the impending fate of the redwoods and brought in a flood of two-dollar contributions to the league. These supplemented the large donations of such men as Stephen Mather, director of the National Park Service, William Kent, and John Phillips of Wenham, Massachusetts, whose gift went for a memorial grove to Colonel Raynal C. Bolling, the first American officer of the upper ranks to be killed in action in World War I.

By 1920, when the league was incorporated as a nonprofit corporation, its membership had topped four thousand, and it had bought four pieces of redwood land along the highway in Humboldt County. Its basic objectives were set: to purchase for a state park the best redwood acreage obtainable along the northern highway, and to preserve as broad a spread of redwood forest as possible, ideally as a national park. The national park goal was not easily realized — Uncle Sam did not seem much interested in the coast redwoods. But if Washington wouldn't help, perhaps Sacramento would. In 1921, the league threw its weight behind a proposal for a $300,000 appropriation to purchase redwood lands. As Robert Shankland described it in his biography, *Steve Mather of the National Parks*, "Under urging, committees from the upper and lower houses (of the legislature) met in joint session. Forceful arguments then unfurled from a throng of persuasive Californians. The joint committee succumbed without much of a struggle and sponsored a bill for $300,000. Word soon circulated, however, that the governor, William D. Stephens, was staring at it doubtfully, and the governor received a visit from the same contingent that had tackled the legislative committee. He said that he could not guarantee approval: The state was poor, the schools were inadequate, and so on. One of the petitioners, William Kent, who had been in Congress with him, leaped to his feet. 'Hell, Bill,' he said, 'shut the schools down. The kids would enjoy it, and it would only take them a year or two to make the work up. If these trees all go, it will take two thousand years to make *them* up.' The governor signed."

Further success attended the Save-the-Redwoods League's legislative efforts in 1927 when the legislature set up the State Park Commission and directed it to make a survey of potential state park areas — a survey which was entrusted to the noted landscape architect Frederick Law Olmsted, Jr., and in 1928 when the state voted a six-million-dollar bond issue so that private contributions for the purchase of park lands would be matched by the state on a dollar-for-dollar basis. In promoting the bond issue, the league was joined by the California Redwood Association and the National Lumber Manufacturers Association — which was symbolic of the generally harmonious relationships the league had succeeded in establishing with the lumber industry with which it dealt.

From the start, the league operated on the principle that the best way to attain its objectives was not to tackle the redwood industry as an enemy, but rather to enlist its cooperation through friendly negotiations. The league's aim was not to save all the redwoods and put the companies out of business, but to preserve enough of the virgin stands so that their perpetuation could be assured and the generations of the future could enjoy their unparalleled beauty. By keeping its objectives limited — and then working patiently but persistently to attain them — the league enhanced its chances of success. And by accepting the premise that the redwood industry should be interfered with to the least extent compatible with the public good, and by standing for fair compensation to those owners whose properties were desired for park purposes, the league won the respect and confidence of the timber operators.

This is not to say that the league's job was easy, or that the lumber people were always altruistic in making the desired lands available. As the league's secretary, former National Parks director Newton B. Drury, wrote recently, ". . . for 45 years the league has been operating just a jump ahead of the sawmills as far as money-raising and land acquisition are concerned, and the state has been limited in appropriated funds that could be applied to land planning." Sometimes the knowledge that the league was interested in a given section of land merely spurred the owner to log it off. Today, state park holdings in the redwood country are almost everywhere hedged in by logging right up to their edges, in what looks suspiciously like a calculated plan to block the parks' future expansion. On the other hand, there have been numerous instances where lumber operators have held off cutting portions of their land wanted by the league, and have been generous in giving the league time to raise the purchase funds (while *they* raised the price). For instance, the Simpson Redwood Company refrained from logging some of its lands adjacent to Jedediah Smith State Park until purchase could be arranged, as did The Pacific Lumber Company with respect to some magnificent stands in the Pepperwood flats that were recently acquired as an extension of the Avenue of the Giants. Both these tracts were generally assumed by the motorist who drove through them to be already a part of the parks.

In its 50 years, the league has succeeded in acquiring and has helped save as state parks 107,729 acres in the redwood belt, including some of the finest virgin stands, with the understanding that the state will "preserve their naturalness, enhance their beauty, and increase their usefulness and inspiration to nature-lovers all over the world." To buy these lands the league raised over $14,000,000, most of which was matched by the state. It is estimated that it would cost more than $250,000,000 to purchase the same tracts at today's inflated prices. The league's present master plan aims at the eventual preservation of 125,000 acres of redwoods, or less than 7 per cent of the original stand, which seems moderate enough when one considers that had it been possible to save all the redwoods the area thus preserved would still have been smaller than the size of New York State's Adirondack Park.

Included in the total acreage now in redwood state parks are numerous smaller groves, many of them of first quality, in Monterey, Santa Cruz, San Mateo, Marin, Sonoma, Mendocino, and Humboldt counties. These range in size from 12 acres in Mendocino's Paul M. Dimmick Memorial Grove, through Richardson Grove's 831 acres in Humboldt County to Samuel P. Taylor State Park's 2,576 acres in Marin County. (Only a small part of the latter includes redwoods.) The five principal redwood parks are the Big Basin Redwoods (expanded to 11,886 acres from the first redwood park established in the Santa Cruz Mountains in 1902); the Humboldt Redwoods State Park (42,318 acres); the Prairie Creek Redwoods State Park on the Humboldt-Del Norte county line (12,241 acres); and the Del Norte Coast Redwoods (6,375 acres) and the Jedediah Smith Redwoods State Park (8,852 acres) in Del Norte County.

Each of the redwood parks has a character of its own. Humboldt Redwoods includes a series of memorial groves along the Redwood Highway, among them the superb Franklin K. Lane Memorial Grove, the Bolling Memorial Grove, and others honoring the memory of a prominent individual. Then there is the Children's Forest, most gifts to which have been made in memory of children who have died; this grove is a fairyland of trees and ferns, meadows and streams, paths and bridges that would enchant any child. Also in Humboldt Redwoods State Park are several larger tracts of virgin redwoods in which the three-hundred-foot colossi form pure stands. These are the "cathedral groves" par excellence; this is the forest to dwarf all other forests. Along Canoe Creek stands the grove named for the Garden Club of America, which, along with the Native Daughters of the

Golden West and the California Federation of Women's Clubs, has been among the league's most generous contributors. Facing each other across the freeway and the South Fork of the Eel, near its confluence with the main Eel River, are the Dyerville Flat, a stand of unusually tall trees including the Founders' Tree, and, possibly the most sublime of them all, Bull Creek Flat, preservation of which was made possible through the gift by John D. Rockefeller, Jr., of $1,000,000 outright and a second $1,000,000 to match other private gifts. Finally, running through the Humboldt Redwoods is that incomparable stretch of two-lane highway, the Avenue of the Giants. The road tunnels through the soaring trees and is best driven, slowly and reverently, in an open-top car.

The Prairie Creek Redwoods, as a league report describes them, differ "widely in character from that of the redwood forest of southern Humboldt County with its heavy 'flats' of virgin redwoods along the river bottoms. The Prairie Creek forest combines both the 'flat' type with the 'slope' type, affording splendid examples of both. The 'slope' timber is unusual in quality, size, and density of stand, and the forest cover very luxuriant. Numerous varieties of ferns, notably the great sword ferns and the delicate lomaria, grow in almost tropical abandon, and rhododendron, huckleberry, and other shrubs. . . . The clover-like oxalis thickly carpets the forest floor and in spring is richly embroidered with patches of wild iris, purple and yellow violets, delicate white trilliums, and redwood lilies. In late May the deep rose rhododendron bursts into its rich flamboyant bloom. In the midst of the woods are many venerable western maples, the branches and trunks of which are entirely moss covered. The silver fir, a symmetrical and beautiful conifer, is found here. . . ." And so is one of the last surviving herds in California of the Roosevelt elk, a large and handsome member of the deer family, which can often be seen grazing in the broad prairie just south of the park headquarters. The park also includes breathtaking sections of wild ocean beach, backed by the abrupt, 250-foot high Gold Bluffs — one of the finest unspoiled stretches of seashore in the country. Recently the Save-the-Redwoods League succeeded in extending the park to include the whole length of beach and bluffs, and with them idyllic Fern Canyon, the perpendicular walls of which are completely tapestried with fronds of five-finger fern.

Farther north, Del Norte Coast Redwoods State Park also adjoins the ocean and offers spectacular views of surf and rocks. Here the redwoods grow on slopes almost right down to the ocean shore, and the understory of rhododendrons is specially flamboyant. Still farther up, near Crescent City, lies Jedediah Smith Redwoods State Park, named after the first white man to lead an expedition to the Pacific through this northwestern corner of California. To some, this is the most beautiful of all the redwood parks. Containing one of the most heavily timbered tracts in the world, it includes the National Tribute Grove, honoring the men and women who served in the U.S. armed forces in World War II, and the Frank D. Stout Memorial Grove at the confluence of the Smith River and Mill Creek. Without question, Mill Creek is one of the most exquisite streams in all the Redwood region. The old Crescent City-Grants Pass stagecoach road winds its unhurried way through some of the finest portions of the reserve, which is also traversed by the Redwood Highway.

These, then, are the Redwoods that were reprieved from the axe and the mindless demands of the market. Ably administered, with an eye to the preservation of their unique natural qualities, by the California State Division of Beaches and Parks, these virgin groves stand in mute tribute to the foresight and tenacity of the Save-the-Redwoods League, without which most of them would have been reduced to stumps and sawlogs. They also stand in tribute to the people of the state of California and to their representatives in Sacramento, who allocated tax monies for the preservation of these trees. They stand, too, as eloquent monuments to the aesthetic sense of tens of thousands of Americans who contributed to their preservation out of the conviction that such a treasure must be saved for all time.

It is moving, as one travels through the flickering light and shade of the Redwood Highway, to realize that many of these groves were given, in part at least, by people who have never seen the redwoods and perhaps do not expect ever to see them. For the members of some of the sponsoring organizations live in Iowa or Vermont, in Georgia or New York. The great majority of them are probably not persons of wealth at all. They gave anonymously, they gave purely, they gave to the future, to people yet unborn; they gave not only to the country but to the world. And they gave out of a deep religious feeling that the beauty and age and greatness that here have risen from the earth to tower above us are holy and shall not be profaned.
— DONALD CULROSS PEATTIE

JAMES ROSE: *Streamside detail, Prairie Creek*

Generations have trod, have trod, have trod;
And all is seared with trade; bleared, smeared with toil;
And wears man's smudge and shares man's smell: the soil
Is bare now, nor can foot feel, being shod.
And for all this, nature is never spent;
There lives the dearest freshness deep down things.
— GERARD MANLEY HOPKINS, "God's Grandeur"

JAMES ROSE: *Bankside, the Emerald Mile, Redwood Creek*

JAMES ROSE: *Licorice fern, Little Lost Man Creek*

JAMES ROSE: *Shelf fungi, Prairie Creek*

Glory be to God for dappled things ...
All things counter, original, spare, strange;
*   Whatever is fickle, freckled (who knows how?)*
*   With swift, slow; sweet, sour; adazzle, dim;*
He fathers-forth whose beauty is past change;
*   Praise him.*

— GERARD MANLEY HOPKINS, "Pied Beauty"

JAMES ROSE: *Forest detail, Prairie Creek*

JAMES ROSE: *Streamside alders, Boyes Creek*

JAMES ROSE: *Mosses, Prairie Creek*

Degged with dew, dappled with dew
Are the groins of the braes that the brook treads through . . .

GORDON ROBINSON: *Trout, Lost Man Creek*

JAMES ROSE: *Stream detail, Prairie Creek*

JAMES ROSE: *Forest detail, Prairie Creek*

JAQUELYN GOODRICH: *Snowfall, Mill Creek*

What would the world be, once bereft
Of wet and of wildness? Let them be left,

N ADAMS: *Streamside, Redwood Creek*

O let them be left, wildness and wet;
Long live the weeds and the wilderness yet.
— GERARD MANLEY HOPKINS, "Inversnaid"

JAMES ROSE: *Spider's work, Lost Man Creek*

HOWARD KING: *Ossagon Road, Prairie Creek*

7. HOW SAFE
ARE THE "SAVED"?

O NE PHRASE recurs like a leitmotif in almost every book or article that mentions the redwood state parks. These trees, the writers like to say, have been "preserved for all time." It is a pleasant thought, a comforting thought. One feels he need worry no longer about the fate of these ancient redwoods. And it is certainly with the assumption that once saved from the woodsman's axe the trees *would* be preserved for all time that thousands of Americans have contributed toward their purchase. Tragically, their faith has been betrayed. Directly or indirectly, we have caused many of these great trees to be *lost* for all time. And many more stand on the brink of destruction.

The tragedy of Bull Creek is an object lesson and a warning of what may yet befall other Redwoods whose perpetual preservation is usually taken for granted. Bull Creek Basin is a watershed some 41 square miles, or 26,000 acres, in area, which rises from 130 feet to 3400 at its highest ridge. Its canyons are deep-cleft, its slopes steep. Its thin soils, derived primarily from Franciscan sediments dating from the late Jurassic or early Upper Cretaceous period, are weak and susceptible to erosion. Heavy rains drench the basin every winter. And yet, over the eons, nature had succeeded in establishing a perfect balance between the forces of rainfall and drought, of fire and erosion, of life and growth. The chaparral forests on the ridge tops, the Douglas firs of the upper slopes, the mixed Douglas fir and redwood of the middle slopes and upper canyons, and the pure coast redwood forests of the flats all lived in harmony with each other and their environment. Their roots anchored the slopes and drained the subsoil. Clear and unsullied, the creeks tumbled from the canyons and widened into placid streams that meandered through the flatlands, their banks graced by maples and alder, dogwoods and willows. Salmon thrashed their waters and spawned in the gravels, and in the spring the young would gather strength for their swim to the ocean.

"To be sure, erosion did occur," wrote James P. Tryner, an officer of the California Division of Beaches and Parks. "But its scars were minimized and quickly healed by the growth of plant life, so that, at any given time, the overall aspect of the landscape was one of stability, of permanence and of beauty. Fires were not unknown in the basin, but when they did occur, there was little surface disturbance of the soil, so that the accelerated erosion which followed found no artificial scars in which to work, and so that the materials which were carried away were largely from the upper layers of the earth, leaving the basic structures of the soils intact to encourage and support returning vegetation.

"Surely, major floods did occur, and indeed, evidence found in the flats below shows that 18 seasons of excessively heavy run-off were experienced in the period between the years 1058 and 1958; an average of one flood every 50 years. But were these periodic floods accompanied by corresponding periods of loss and destruction in the forest? Apparently not, for the evidence shows that immediately following each flood the forests in the flats experienced a period of accelerated growth, apparently brought on by the deposition of silt eroded from the top soil levels of the upper basin."

The entire basin, then, formed an ecological unity, and all its components — the trees, the streams, the climate and soil — were interrelated and interdependent. The incomparable forest in Bull Creek Flat, known today as the Rockefeller Forest, did not owe its splendor to factors existing in the flats alone, but was the end product, the climactic achievement of forces at work in the watershed as a whole. Alas this was realized too late. The preservation of Bull Creek Flat became one of the very earliest objectives of the Save-the-Redwoods League, and with the help of John D. Rockefeller, Jr., was achieved in 1931. But only the choicest area was bought—9400 acres in the flats and on the immediately adjacent slopes. The rest of Bull Creek basin remained in private hands. In 1947, large-scale logging began in the Bull Creek watershed. And this was logging that ranked with the worst, perpetrated by typical cut and get out operators with no care or understanding of the land. These loggers stripped the steep slopes, gutted the canyons, gouged the hills with skid trails and roads. The soil, denuded of its protective trees, reverted to its basic instability, and became easy prey to the winter downpours. The sparkling streams grew dull and muddy; they burst their banks and spread ever wider. Soon the salmon and steelhead were gone from Bull Creek. And still the logging proceeded, unnoticed by the public. By 1954 more than half of the watershed had been laid bare. And between 1950 and 1955, fires completed the devastation of some 7,000 acres.

In a few short years, man, in his blind and greedy compulsion to turn trees into dollars, had brutally upset the delicate balance that nature had built up over the ages. Then in December 1955, torrential rains fell on the Bull Creek watershed, and the tragic damage that man had done became immediately apparent. In the upper basin, vast slides dumped millions of yards of rock and gravel into the streams, to be carried down towards the flats below. Stream banks were eroded at the base and slid into the creeks. These became roaring torrents flowing on broad expanses of raw gravel. In the period of a few hours, raging waters ripped through the Rockefeller Forest, toppling more than 300 major trees (trees in excess of four feet in diameter, breast high) into Bull Creek's channel and washing away 50 acres of land from the flats themselves. Debris and logs piled up in the creek channel until at one point there was a log jam 40 feet high, which completely choked the stream. Protective vegetation was torn from the banks, and an additional 99 trees were undercut so badly that later they had to be felled before clean-up work in the creek could begin. Enormous quantities of debris, silt and gravel were deposited in the flats at the base of the trees, and these deposits, unlike the naturally-occurring accumulations of silt of ages past, were not beneficial but led to the later death of many trees.

The damage was not confined to that one great storm of the winter of 1955–56. Every rainy season since then the toll of trees has grown, more than 500 giant redwoods having fallen as a result of the flood of 1955. In 1964 a storm rivaling that of 1955 took away nearly 400 more trees. The undercutting of the banks continues, and the spreading of the gravel that strangles the plant life along the streams. Bull Creek is no longer the beautiful stream it once was. Where it flows through the flats, it has been widened by erosion from an original width of 50 to 100 feet to widths approaching 300 feet in many places, and the huge quantities of raw gravel deposited in it have raised the level of its bed an estimated five feet.

The Division of Beaches and Parks is scrambling to protect the Rockefeller Forest from further damage. Bulldozers are at work in the stream bed of Bull Creek, deepening the channel through the gravel. Dump trucks drive up and spill their load of rocks down the raw banks to halt the undercutting action of the stream. A system of checkdams is planned in the upper basin to arrest the movement of gravel downstream. Above all, it was realized that as long as a large part of the watershed remained in private hands the protection enjoyed by the state park lands was illusory, and the Save-the-Redwoods League has been buying up the private holdings and deeding them over to the state in a program of acquisition now more than three-quarters completed. Treated as an ecological unity, protected from fire and logging, helped where necessary by artificial re-vegetation and channel control work, the Bull Creek Basin will in time heal itself. But the trees that were toppled are gone, and Bull Creek will not recover its full beauty.

If the Bull Creek tragedy has taught us anything, it is the necessity to consider the whole ecological setting of any area that we may desire to preserve in its natural condition. This is particularly true in the redwood region with its heavy precipitation and unstable soils. The redwood parks are not islands, and they can and will be damaged by logging and fires and other destruction occurring beyond their boundaries but within the same watersheds. The parks, to be really protected, must include whole watersheds and this is not the case at present. Jedediah Smith, for instance, includes only the lower portion of Mill Creek; most of the stream's watershed is still in private hands, and a big new sawmill has been erected upstream from the park. Here the terrain is not as steep as in Bull Creek basin and the soils are less erosible. It is to be hoped that the loggers will be more cautious in their operations. But the rainfall is even heavier than in Humboldt County. At the very least, we may expect that upstream logging will soil Mill Creek's pristine beauty (some muddying already has been reported).

The implications of the Bull Creek lesson are of nationwide importance. The

EDGAR WAYBURN: *Crossing Redwood Creek*

JAMES ROSE: *Ossagon Creek, near Gold Bluffs beach*

need to preserve a region's ecological integrity applies just as well to the Grand Canyon or the Everglades. And the Bull Creek experience has ethical and legal aspects that transcend the redwoods. Who was primarily hurt by the loggers' and timber owners' rape of the Bull Creek basin? Not the loggers and the timber owners but the owners of the Rockefeller Forest — i.e., the people of the state of California. Who is paying to repair the devastated land? Again, not the loggers and the timber owners who ruined it, but the people of California. "Under our present criminal code," writes Fairfield Osborn in *Our Plundered Planet*, "anyone who steals food from a groceryman's counter can be put in jail. His act hurts only the proprietor of the store. But if, for the benefit of his own pocketbook, the owner of timberlands at the head of a river strips the hills of their forests, the net result is that food is taken not from one 'proprietor' but from all the 'proprietors,' or farm owners, down the valley, because the removal of forest cover on an upper watershed will inevitably damage the water supply in the valley below, even to the point of causing the complete drying-up of wells and springs. Countless thousands of landowners in America have in this very way been brought to bankruptcy. In the face of such things, how equitable are our present moral codes?"

In the case of Bull Creek, the devastation of the upper watershed caused no drying-up downstream — rather the opposite. But Osborn's principle is still valid. And in this case, the loggers took no food from their downstream victims. But they took something more precious, because it is rare and irreplaceable: they marred the beauty of an area that has few equals in the world. And they marred it not just for today's proprietors down the valley, they marred it for all time — for all future Californians and Americans and foreign visitors who will never see Bull Creek Flat quite as beautiful as it once was. But were the owners of the devastated lands in the upper Bull Creek watershed — or the lumber operators they employed — ever called to account? Were they ever sued for the damages they caused to the Rockefeller Forest? Were they ever even required to repair their own lands so that future harm to the state park could be minimized? Far from it. They made a nice profit on the lumber cut — and then demanded a tidy sum before they would part with their cut-over lands. Until the Forest Practice Act is so strengthened that a landowner or logger will think twice before stripping the land — because he will be required to repair it at his own expense, and will be held financially liable for any damages which his misuse of the land may cause others — there will be something rotten in the state of California, and no redwood park that does not include a complete watershed can ever be considered to be truly preserved.

This much can perhaps be said in favor of the perpetrators of the Bull Creek tragedy: They did not foresee the end results of their logging practices. They did not set out deliberately to ruin Bull Creek Flat.

But the highly trained, efficient, methodical and forward-planning operatives of the California State Division of Highways know what they are doing — and they do it just the same.

On August 28, 1960, Governor Edmund G. Brown of California stood up before a throng of notables seated in the shadow of the redwoods along the Avenue of the Giants, rested his fists on a lectern improvised from a redwood stump, and spoke into the microphones as follows:

"I am privileged to speak for 15½ million Californians as we dedicate the first stage of a parkway which will lead through one of the most beautiful parts of California and the world. . . .

"We are following definite principles in our freeway program in these matchless areas. A basic premise is to open up new vistas to Californians, and our millions of visitors from other states and nations. Engineering considerations, which make this possible, are important. But it is equally sound state policy to retain scenic beauty in the unspoiled wilderness as we route freeways through the state park areas.

"What we have done here will be done elsewhere in the redwoods — at Prairie Creek, Jedediah Smith and Richardson Grove. . . ."

God forbid!

For what was done was to spoil the wilderness; to open up new vistas that never should have been opened up; and to route freeways through the state park areas when by all standards of ethics such areas should have been off limits to the highway division's bulldozers and graders. [By 1964, the freeway dispute had moved Governor Brown to the point that he promised that no more redwoods would be cut to accommodate freeways; a promise, unfortunately, he was in no position to keep.]

Through parts of Humboldt Redwoods State Park there now run two parallel roadways. One is the old Redwood Highway, now renamed the Avenue of the Giants Parkway. Along this you may still drive at a leisurely pace, your eyes straining upward through your windshield to gauge the height of the trees, whose branches often meet overhead. The traffic here is light, and it is easy to pull off the road and to step out of your car to enjoy the beauty and the quiet of the forest. But no sooner is your motor stopped than you become aware that there is no real silence here. The swish of speeding cars, the roar of lumber trucks rudely intrude upon your reverie. You look up the slope towards the source of the noise — and through a thin screen of trees you see the shapes of the cars and trucks speeding along the neighboring freeway.

The old highway almost tunnels through the forest, opening a minimum rift in the canopy overhead. It does no violence to the harmony of the landscape. From the air it is visible only when viewed from points in line with the highway's direction. The freeway is something else again. A four-lane, high-speed structure with a minimum of curves and grades, it cuts a brutal swath through the trees. "Construction of the freeway involved heavy clearing and the use of heavy logging equipment," says a 1962 issue of *California Highways and Public Works* magazine. "The freeway traverses rugged and heavily wooded terrain." In places the slopes were gouged to many times the freeway's width with cuts and fills to

ANN ADAMS: *Humboldt Redwoods State Park forest*

prevent landslides. At one point the old highway was only a 20-foot niche in the side of a mountain. But the 60-foot freeway required a huge cut into the hill. This Big Cut, as it is known, is hundreds of feet high and required the excavation of 1,400,000 cubic yards of dirt and rock and the felling of hundreds of giant redwoods. Where the freeway adjoins the rivers, the natural aspect of the banks has been forever ruined. "Needless to say, considerable bank protection was involved in this 'man versus rivers' phase of the project," states another article in *California Highways.* "Combinations of heavy stone rip-rap, grouted rock, slope paving, and timber pile jetties were designed to protect new fills and turn back the rivers at points of impingement." All this and unspoiled wilderness too?

Indeed the freeway does open up new vistas — at the cost of irreparable damage to the river valley forest and serious storm blowdown peril to the roadside trees. And the vistas are in no way comparable to those offered by the old road. Instead of the forest closing in on all sides, majestic, mysterious, and overpowering, the trees along the freeway seem to recede into the distance, brushed aside and diminished in stature by the wide expanses of pavement and bare earth and sky, and the unique redwoods become no more impressive than a forest of any other evergreen species.

For engineering and economic reasons, the Division of Highways found it convenient to route the freeway through portions of Humboldt Redwoods State Park — the route was more direct, and since the park lands were already owned by the state, right-of-way acquisition costs were held to a minimum. Some concession was made to aesthetics by skirting some of the finer groves in the flats, and building the freeway on the slopes above them. Unfortunately even there it is damaging the forest below — damaging it not only aesthetically, by destroying its tranquility, but physically as well. There are indications that the freeway is acting as a dam, interrupting the normal downhill seepage of groundwater and nutrients to the trees below. Many of these may be doomed as a result.

The parks father north — Prairie Creek, Del Norte, and Jedediah Smith — have not yet been invaded by the freeway. But proposed freeways have stood as threats now for half a dozen years. A freeway route has actually been adopted across the northern end of Jedediah Smith park. It would tear a wide swath through some of the finest groves adjoining the Smith River. The route was adopted with the concurrence of the Division of Beaches and Parks, which, feeling powerless then, was willing to accept a freeway if the worst possible routing was not chosen. Later, the Division learned the public expected it to stand up to fight for the integrity of the parkland entrusted to it. Evenually, the State Park Commission urged the State Highway Commission to find an alternate route outside the park. A more costly, but feasible, route exists north of the park. After a number of years, the Highway Commission has failed to make any change in its route adoption, though studies continue. It is to be hoped that inclusion of the area in a Redwood National Park will permanently block any freeway in this location.

HOWARD KING: *Fern Canyon*

While an apparent victory has been won with respect to blunting a freeway threat aimed at Prairie Creek State Park, that problem has also not been definitely resolved. The battle of Prairie Creek was the turning point in the showdown between the Division of Beaches and Parks and the Division of Highways. Beaches and Parks did not agree to any of the proposed routes through the park. None of the four alternatives was acceptable, as each would destroy the integrity of an intact forest-and-seashore parkland that reaches a width of nearly four miles. One route would have barreled along the shore destroying the marvelous wild beach. Another would have run just to the east, along the top of Gold Bluffs. This route would drive a permanent scar all the way through the park between beach and redwood forest areas, and would span or fill exquisite Fern Canyon and other natural pathways between the shore and hinterland. Widening the present highway to freeway standards would have ruined Prairie Creek itself and the best of the forest. And bringing a freeway inside the eastern edge of the park would have meant the end of some of the quietest and most beautiful dedicated groves, and would have required the typical hideous fills and cuts.

The public backed the Division in its defense of the park. Ultimately, Governor Brown prevailed upon the Highway Commission to undertake a search for a satisfactory route which would avoid the park. There is an alternative route that would detour around the park to the east, passing entirely through logged-over land. This route would be more expensive, as it is slightly longer and would pass through private lands, thus presenting more difficulties in acquisition than would be involved in preëmpting park land. But it would offer no insuperable construction problems, it would actually benefit the park by routing fast through traffic and noisy logging and lumber trucks around it, and if the park's integrity is to be preserved this is the only acceptable route. While the Division of Highways' studies of this route have been underway for a number of years, no specific route has been finally adopted. Again National Park status may take the decision out of the state's hands.

Compared with the Division of Beaches and Parks, the Division of Highways has almost unlimited funds. And until recently it possessed practicallly carte blanche to bulldoze its freeways wherever it wished. It enjoys powers of eminent domain and of immediate taking, and any decision of the Highway Commission as to the public necessity of a given freeway has been by law conclusive. In any showdown, Beaches and Parks have been clearly outmatched. There is a fine stand of virgin redwoods west of Pepperwood for which the Save-the-Redwoods League and the state parks authorities had been negotiating as an addition to the Avenue of the Giants and a memorial to Dag Hammarskjold, and which the lumber company had reserved from logging. But without even checking with the league or the Division of Beaches and Parks, the Division of Highways acquired a right-of-way for an extension of the freeway that would completely obliterate the western portion of this stand.

In 1968, however, the Legislature granted the Division of Beaches and Parks the power to contest a route selection through a park, and a procedure has been worked out to insure that the Division of Beaches and Parks is consulted in advance of such selection. How much this change will tip the scales remains to be seen. The 1965 Federal Aid Highway Act, in addition, admonished states to route freeways around parks wherever feasible by-passes can be found (this admonition was weakened, however, in 1968).

Ethics, as well as esthetics, are involved in the freeway threat to the redwood parks. The thousands of Americans who contributed to the Save-the-Redwoods League did not intend the acres purchased with their donations to be used to speed traveling salesmen and logging trucks between Oregon and Ukiah. They gave to save redwoods, and to save them for all time. And the state of California, in accepting title to and assuming the administration of the redwood parks, also assumed the obligation to protect and preserve them — from fire, from logging, *and* from the freeways. Considerations of engineering and economics are secondary to this trust. There is no ethical justification for one mile of freeway in the redwood parks: in allowing the freeway to pass through Humboldt Redwoods State Park, the state of California has been guilty of a breach of trust.

The league has received many letters of protest, even of resignation, from members who have been outraged by this breach of trust. "Why contribute money to buy land that will be despoiled by the highway department of the state?" asked one member. "In California where you have these redwood forests I fail to see why you can't secure the coöperation of the highway department to run their roads elsewhere."

Another correspondent wrote: "I am not renewing my membership in the Save-the-Redwoods League, because properties purchased through your organization go into the state park system — with whose 'protection' I have become thoroughly disillusioned.

"What is the point of contributing to purchase of property back of Palm Springs for a 'wild area,' only to have the state authorize a commercial tramway into it — effectively destroying the character of the 'preserved' area?

"What is the point of contributing indirectly to Bliss State Park at Tahoe — only to have the state highway department insist on a bridge across Emerald Bay that will destroy that?

"I am sorry not to contribute again to you, but the state of California has welched on the understandings that existed when contributions have been made to 'preserve inviolate for all time these natural areas' — and until I am convinced that there will be no more fraud and deception, even if the bad faith is by other divisions of the state than the park system, I have no intention of making any more contributions where the state of California is concerned.

"I do not think I am alone in feeling this way."

Indeed he is not. There is a growing feeling in the state that too much beauty is being sacrificed to the internal combustion engine; that too often, because it has the funds and must answer to no one on how they are spent, the Division of

Highways scars the land with its freeways where there is no need for them; that the division should obtain its funds through legislative appropriations like all other divisions of the state government; and that the Highway Commission should be required to clear its plans with men whose eye for the landscape encompasses more than the gradient of a slope or the radius of a curve. There is a feeling, in short, that the all-powerful highway commission must be curbed before the state strangles in the tentacles of its freeways.

Besides the thousands of "preserved" redwoods that have fallen victim to the freeway or to erosion caused by logging, there are many more that are threatened by another kind of erosion: human erosion. In the long run, the trees' best friends could do them harm — the people who love the redwoods enough to drive out to see them, who like to camp beneath the great trees and hike the shadowy trails.

Already in several of the parks there is evidence that the trees are suffering from too much compaction of the soil over their shallow root systems. The growing throng of admirers who park their cars and set up their tents and walk about in the groves is slowly but surely destroying the trees. The undergrowth suffers too, to the extent that in certain areas it has practically disappeared.

This wear and tear is becoming more serious all the time, as the popularity of the redwoods increases, as the population itself grows, and as people enjoy more and more leisure time and are increasingly inclined to spend their leisure in travel and outdoor recreation. Every year the campgrounds in the redwood parks become more crowded. The qualities of silence and mystery and solitude that are essential components of the redwoods' magic become increasingly impaired. The state parks administrators have successfully resisted pressures for cheap and tawdry development of the redwood parklands. But they must try to meet the growing public's legitimate demands for campgrounds and parking areas and toilets and trails.

The answer to this population pressure, obviously, is to expand the parks. In part, this will require the acquisition of enough additional virgin timber so that future generations may, despite their greater numbers, still find among the redwoods something of those qualities that we can enjoy today. It will also require the acquisition of cut-over lands adjacent to today's parks, which would serve a double purpose. Protected from the continuous logging that will be standard practice on private lands, these cut-over lands will heal themselves and in a century or two should be clothed with fine stands of large trees. Provided the parks are rounded out to include whole watersheds, then these second-growth areas would protect from erosion the superlative stands in the original parks. And they could also protect them from the mounting human erosion: campgrounds and related facilities could be shifted away from the virgin stands and into the rehabilitated sections, which for those purposes would be highly acceptable substitutes.

The alternative to expanding the parks will have to be the rationing of admissions — put your name down on the list and wait until it is called two or three or five years later, as Secretary of the Interior Stewart L. Udall warned at the Wilderness Conference in San Francisco in March 1963. Speaking of our uncontrolled proliferation and of its predictable effect on our scenic resources, he said: ". . . certain aspects of the problem are already evident. They are particularly evident here in California, where population growth is seemingly a public business of considerable pride. The San Francisco Bay Area is a prime example. Studies by the U.S. Department of Commerce indicate that the population of this region will not merely double but almost quadruple within 60 years. For every person presently living in this area, according to the statisticians, there will be three others alongside him. Will there be four times as many automobiles on the freeways? Or will there be four times as many freeways? . . .

"Of one thing we can be absolutely certain: There will not be four times as much open space available to the residents of this region. There will not be four times as many parks. . . . [And] it is a fact that if the population quadruples, we can expect that there will be far more than four times as much *demand* for open spaces, for parks, for wilderness. . . . We can consider the possibility that a quadrupled population will demand at least nine times as much outdoor recreation — nine times as much wilderness for hiking, fishing, camping, and ironically, for 'solitude.'

"Under these conditions, for every person who now hopes to camp in the summertime on the floor of Yosemite Valley, there will be an eventual nine. For every present hiker down the John Muir Trail along the spine of the Sierra, there will be nine. For every tin can and bottle and carton that now litters park and wilderness trails, there will be nine. For every hundred people on the beach at Drake's Bay, there will be at least 900 and conceivably several times that many. Here we have, in dramatic and depressing terms, the geography of rising population."

Will there be nine times as many people who will want to explore and camp in the Redwood parks? Quite possibly. But we cannot hope to save nine times as many trees as have now been set aside — there just is not that much virgin growth left. We can save more than we have, however. And indeed we must, if those trees already saved are to be "preserved for all time."

JAMES ROSE: *Grove above Elam Creek*

JAMES ROSE: *Detail, forest floor, Lost Man Creek*

8. EPILOGUE—OR EPITAPH

TALL AND STRAIGHT the last redwoods stand, while we debate their fate. They are our captives; their death has been decreed. There still is time to stay the execution — but time is running short. If we debate too long we will discover that the executioner has taken the decision from our hands: his axe will have claimed those lives we could have spared.

It is somehow preposterous that we of this generation — we of this decade, even — should have the power to reprieve or condemn a race that nature has preserved over more than 100,000,000 years. There is something frighteningly presumptuous about a man, his life span limited to a few decades, who strides up to a redwood that has seen a thousand summers and might see as many more, and in an hour's hacking and sawing brings the giant down.

Indeed there are many who feel that any further logging of virgin redwood is simply immoral, and would stop using redwood and look for substitutes rather than complete the destruction of these incomparable trees. One such citizen was Madison Grant, who wrote: "It is scarcely necessary to dwell on the crime involved in the destruction of the oldest trees on earth. The cutting of a sequoia for grape stakes or railroad ties is like breaking up one's grandfather's clock for kindling to save the trouble of splitting logs at the woodpile, or lighting one's pipe with a Greek manuscript to save the trouble of reaching for the matches.

"After the fall of the Roman Empire the priceless works of classic art were 'needed' for lime, and statues were slacked down for this purpose, but the men who did it are today rightly dubbed 'vandals and barbarians.' What then will the next generation call us if we continue to destroy these priceless trees because lumber is 'needed' for grape stakes and railroad ties?"

If by some freak we were to come across, in some hitherto unexplored corner of the world, a surviving herd of dinosaurs, a species contemporary with the earliest redwoods, would we seek to preserve it or would we kill it off for its hides or its meat or its carcasses? Quite possibly the latter, for it has always been man's bent to reduce nature's myriad marvels to their lowest common denominator — human "needs." And he has always justified this attitude with the self-serving assumption that God made the earth for man to enjoy. What man finds useful is by definition good. What he has no use for is worthless and probably evil. "What good is it?" (meaning "What good is it to *me*?") asks man as he brings his heel down on a toad in his garden — although the toad may consume the insects that attack his flowers.

Because we are clever, we find ever new ways to push nature around so as to fit her to our needs. Because we are not clever enough, or foresighted enough, to halt the multiplication of our numbers, we find we have ever greater needs to meet and must push nature that much harder. And so we make constantly increasing demands on the resources of our nonexpanding planet. We remake our landscape to conform to man-made patterns. And what it gains in usefulness it loses in diversity and beauty.

The Southwest "needs" more power for its booming population — and the fantastically beautiful gorge of Glen Canyon is dammed and drowned in silty water; other dams have been proposed that would mutilate Grand Canyon itself. But does the Southwest really need these extra millions of citizens? The San Francisco Bay Area "needs" more land for homes and industry — and one of the world's great bays shrinks yearly as its shallows are filled. Northern California "needs" a new freeway to accommodate growing motor traffic between San Francisco and Crescent City, and thousands of irreplaceable redwoods are sacrificed to the automobile.

Often the so-called needs are spurious — mere creations of promotion and advertising. Paris couturiers decree that the well-dressed woman "needs" a coat of Somali leopard. And while the magnificent beasts are exterminated the women's pages unblushingly feature the pelts, the furriers stock them, and women buy them. It matters little that a woman can be both warm and chic in a coat made of some material that does not threaten a species with extinction. Advertising and promotion — and the undoubted handsomeness of the product — have boomed redwood as a material for sidings and paneling and decks and patios, and redwood houses as a result enjoy a tremendous vogue. Of course homes just as splendid and just as modern are being built of other materials that do not require the chopping down of the world's most beautiful and fastest-dwindling virgin forests.

But man does not live by bread alone. He has needs that are no less real and no less vital — although they are harder to measure in economic terms — than food and water and shelter. He has a thirst for beauty. He often has a hunger for solitude. He craves the companionship of other animal species. He has a deep, atavistic urge for identification with nature. Witness the extraordinary upsurge of hiking and camping and boating and the overwhelming increase in use of our national parks.

Unfortunately, we too often take things for granted until they get scarce. We begin to worry about a bird or an animal only when suddenly we realize it is becoming extinct. Only now, when our unspoiled wilderness is down to isolated fragments, are we beginning to realize how much we miss its former glory, and are we trying to preserve what little is left. Such regrets are frequently too late. We may mourn the demise of the passenger pigeon but nothing will bring it back to life. We might be tempted to dynamite Glen Canyon Dam but it would be too late. The muddy waters impounded behind it have already ruined forever the canyon they drowned. We might wish we could raze Los Angeles'

MARTIN LITTON: *View across lower Redwood Creek*

sprawling suburbs, but whatever else this might accomplish it would not bring back the orange groves.

With the last redwoods, we still have a chance. But to preserve what we already have saved we have to save more. And in fairness to our grandchildren and their grandchildren we have to save still more. Establishment of an adequate Redwood National Park offers us our best and perhaps last chance to preserve for all time an adequate and representative segment of the world's finest forest.

If through indolence, indifference or misguided economy we fail to make the most of this opportunity, our generation, which already has allowed the sacrifice of so much natural beauty to the false gods of growth and progress, will go down in history as the one that allowed the last of the virgin redwoods to be sold down the Eel and the Klamath rivers and Redwood Creek, and converted into commercial products for which substitutes were on hand.

We are grateful for the preservation that was achieved, even though it did not quite come up to the dream. We ourselves may yet earn the gratitude of those to come, *if* we become aroused at the desecration of the world's finest forest, *if* we bring the weight of our collective indignation — our own and that of the government that serves us — to bear, *if* we insist that the ever-living sequoias shall indeed live on.

We are each but an assemblage of atoms, touched briefly with the miracle of awareness, thoughtfulness, and joy. Our time on the planet is short and finite, our capacity for creativity and destruction infinite.

ANN ADAMS: *Yellow bush lupine*

DONALD ANTHROP: *Mussel Point, near mouth of Redwood Creek*

We have enormous obligations: in our hands is the dis-
position of everything alive on earth.

— AL MOLINA

MARTIN LITTON: *Count's Hill Prairie and upper Emerald Mile, Redwood Creek*

THE PARKLAND OF REDWOOD CREEK

by PEGGY WAYBURN

IT IS EASY to pass by Redwood Creek without knowing it is there. Forty miles north of Eureka the Redwood Highway leaves the rim of surf and cuts inland. It travels past a small mill, through pastureland where torn black stumps still stand beneath a grassy hill. A swing to the east, and against the skyline stands a wall of tall dark trees, stormswept, and marked with stark white snags — primeval redwoods. Ahead to the north lies the little town of Orick, strung out a mile along the road — a bright red house, a logger's bar, a school, motels, cows in the field beside a store. Halfway through town, a river slips beneath the highway bridge, its waters caught between the banks of a gray gravel levee. There is no hint that this is one of the major streams of the redwood region, no sign that around the bend to the east lies a great unbroken redwood forest. This is Redwood Creek.

Rising on the wooded slope of South Fork Mountain, Redwood Creek travels fifty-five miles to reach the sea, dropping 5,000 feet, and taking its course north-westerly, parallel to the Mad River and the Eel. Its headwaters cut a rocky channel for many miles along an old fault line, and the river here foams white and wild. In its gentle lower course, the waters meander easily, spread wide among the shifting river bars. It runs through ranch and pastureland, past natural prairies bright with wildflowers in the spring, past dark towering walls of trees. Along the way, four small tributaries swell its flow. From the east come Lacks Creek and Minor Creek, good fishing streams with clear swift riffles. On the west, Devil's Creek and Bridge Creek spill in. And Prairie Creek, almost another river as it gathers the waters of Lost Man and Little Lost Man Creek, pours in near Orick.

The redwoods grow their tallest along the river flats, sometimes higher than 350 feet where the rich alluvial soil is moist, where fogs linger and the shadows are deep. But there are also big trees on the slopes and ridgetops of Redwood Creek. In these higher communities, they grow in a mixed stand with tall firs and spruce and hemlocks. These forests are airier, with a lacy understory of oaks and alders and bursts of dogwood in the spring. Here some redwoods stand alone, solid, straight, and massive. Others stand close together like the pipes of an immense organ. The sun slips through the open forest and the fluted bark glows red-brown or silvery gray. The wind sounds high against the sky, and touches the understory gently. Underfoot, the smaller members of the forest community grow, pink trillium, yellow violets, and the delicate calypso lady-

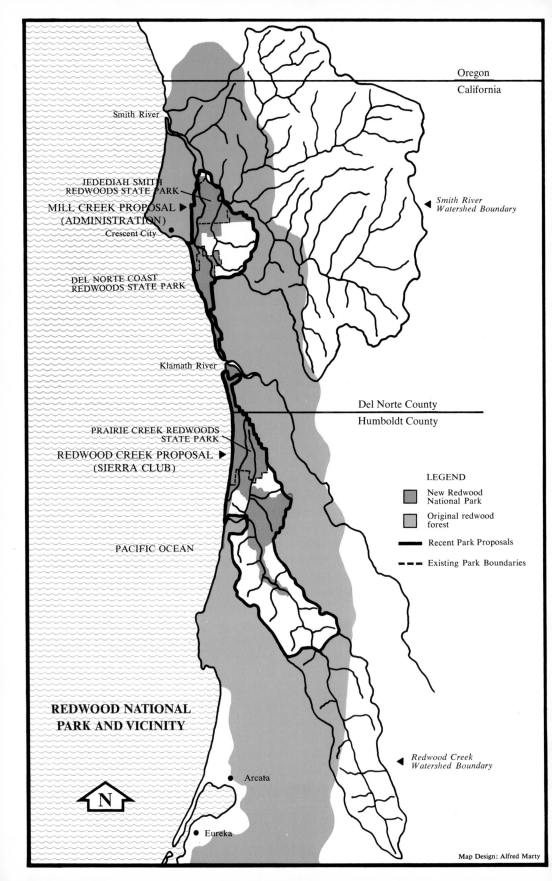

Oregon

California

Smith River

JEDEDIAH SMITH
REDWOODS STATE PARK
MILL CREEK PROPOSAL ▶
(ADMINISTRATION)

Crescent City

◀ *Smith River*
Watershed Boundary

DEL NORTE COAST
REDWOODS STATE PARK

Klamath River

Del Norte County

Humboldt County

PRAIRIE CREEK REDWOODS
STATE PARK

REDWOOD CREEK PROPOSAL ▶
(SIERRA CLUB)

LEGEND

New Redwood
National Park

Original redwood
forest

Recent Park Proposals

Existing Park Boundaries

PACIFIC OCEAN

**REDWOOD NATIONAL
PARK AND VICINITY**

◀ *Redwood Creek*
Watershed Boundary

N

Arcata

Eureka

Map Design: Alfred Marty

slipper orchids now almost extinct in the redwood region. Sword ferns and deer ferns send out their fronds like small green fountains on the slopes. Oxalis, the redwood sorrel, opens to the sun and furls tight in the shade. The forest floor is springy with deep duff laid down through countless centuries, a mosaic of leaves and small cones and needles.

To date, stretches of forest on lower Redwood Creek have survived the natural cataclysms of fire and flood — and man's depredations. It is a vigorous forest, with many strong young trees. A great fire swept through about 600 years ago, leaving black scars on many older giants. But the unscarred trees are almost as tall and broad, and meant to live another thousand years or more.

Close to the sea where the winds are heavy with moisture and the fogs are frequent, the groves of Redwood Creek become a rain-forest of redwoods, hemlocks, spruce, and alders. Mosses grow thick and soft on the bark; tree-ferns drape the heavy limbs, and fallen trees bear young trees whose slender roots reach around the old trunks to find the ground below. The sky is hidden by the heavy forest canopy, the sunlight seeping through to light the big-leaf maples to a green-gold underwater glow. The forest's silence is deeper for the sound of distant surf.

Along the shore, the forest gives way to meadowland and the windswept Gold Bluffs. Roosevelt elk graze in the little meadows along the beach, among the last of the great herds that once roamed all the redwood region. Home Creek cuts through the bluffs in a shadowy canyon draped with five-finger ferns. A few miles to the south, where Redwood Creek leaves its levee, there are mounds of clam shells, left by the Indians who once buried their dead here, within sight of the river and the sea.

The once-forested flats at the mouth of Redwood Creek were cleared long since, and burned — perhaps a hundred years ago — for pastureland and the building of Orick, a stage stop along the Redwood Highway. But the great groves upriver were off the beaten track. They stood while other grand forests went down, the forests of the Salmon, the Elk, the Ah Pah, the Mad, and the accessible reaches of the Klamath, the Smith, and the Eel. The logging of Redwood Creek waited for the 1940's, and did not really get into swing until the '50's. So great was the volume on a single acre of its forest land that logging progressed slowly, even with the modern equipment that lets two men bring down a redwood tree in an hour. It was the country's great good fortune that the topography of Redwood Creek helped to spare the superlative trees and groves growing there — the tallest known tree, and many others of record size.

The unique topography as well as the magnificence of the Redwood Creek groves had been noted—and recommended for national park acquisition—a half century ago. In June, 1920, Madison Grant wrote in the National Geographic Magazine: "At Orick, on the Big Lagoon, the highway passes through the lower end of Redwood Creek grove, one of the very best stands of redwood in Humboldt County...This stand is as yet untouched and should be saved for a national park, because the lumber, being inaccessible, can be acquired at a relatively small cost."

He and Henry Fairfield Osborn and John C. Merriam had recently returned from an adventurous outing into the redwood region to survey the area for a possible national park. Grant went on to comment: "A national park requires a large area, with sufficient isolation and compactness to admit of proper administration. There are three such areas available: 1st, the grove along Redwood Creek…peculiarly adapted for a national park: 2nd, the groves along the Klamath River, as yet untouched and of great beauty: 3rd, the Smith River groves in Del Norte County. (He later mentioned also the groves of the south bank of the Eel River.)

Madison Grant, a man of great vision, did not himself realize fully what the park chance was at Redwood Creek. In his time, no thought was given to the bigger idea of preserving a whole watershed, however compact. The goal then and for many years was the preservation of "large" but separate groves of a few thousand acres, and later, for roadside strips. The complete and compact 240,000 acre watershed of Redwood Creek in 1920 would indeed have made a magnificent national park. It could have embraced a total redwood ecosystem—relatively untouched—from sea to mountaintop, a magnificent sweep from the misty rainforest of the coast to the sunny upland slopes, clear and warm on the foggiest of summer days. It would have included the green prairies studded with wildflowers, the airier slope forests, and all the sweet clear running streams. It would have provided a marvelous variety of pleasure for the millions of people who would one day want —and deserve—the chance to know the redwoods in their full glory. Yet it would have been a relatively small national park, far smaller, say, than the 900,000 acre Olympic National Park which protects the Douglas fir. A quarter-million acres— little enough token to pay a species that had survived for more than a hundred million years before the coming of man.

By the time the National Park Service confirmed Madison Grant's findings by recommending a national park at Redwood Creek in 1964, the world, of course, had changed. Logging had already chewed up portions of the great groves, and was proceeding apace. The upper reaches of the watershed had long since been converted to ranchland and grazed. Since Redwood Creek contained some of the last stands of old growth timber still upright in the Redwood region, the area was considered gold in the coffers of the timber industry, and the industry was not about to give it up. The happy days of acquiring any magnificent grove for a relatively small cost were gone. Already, the great park opportunity was diminished.

Still, the 90,000 acre park at Redwood Creek proposed by the Sierra Club in 1965 would have made a fine park then. This fraction of the watershed included smaller but still sizable watersheds of Lost Man, Little Lost Man, McArthur, Elam, Bridge and Devil's creeks. It included the magnificent unbroken forest lawn that still grew along the east bank of lower Redwood Creek. And it included the creek's ridge-to-ridge watershed above the Emerald Mile. Industry attacked the proposal as a monstrous "land grab" and even certain conservationists considered it too ambitious.

In contrast, the 54,000 acre area proposed by the Park Service for Redwood Creek was modest indeed. Yet even this was deemed to be too much, and the park as established on October 2, 1968, took in only 23,000 acres of the Redwood Creek area. Centered around the lower reaches of the creek, it stretched north along 32 highly scenic miles of the coast and tacked on an addition to Jedediah Smith Redwood State Park in Mill Creek (a watershed of the Smith River). Within its boundaries it included three state parks containing 28,000 acres and some of the finest groves owned by the state of California. Circumscribed by the hard fact that the $92,000,000 authorized to be spent—a record for any national park— could only stretch so far, it was acknowledgedly a compromise park. Since powerful interests wanted no park at all, its establishment was a decided conservation victory.

But whether that victory will be pyrrhic remains to be seen. Congress was well aware of the limitations of the compromise park at the time it was established. It was a fragmented park of many separate units, difficult to develop, to administer, and hard for the visitor to comprehend. There were few extensive trails for hikers and backpackers that could be located through areas that were not threatened by future logging. Along existing roads, visitors were repeatedly shocked by the scars of clear-cutting. Thus, it became the stated hope of many people, including congressmen and senators, that a part or all of many areas contiguous to the park could be added to improve the visitor's experience.

Congress, moreover, attempted to minimize the limitations of the compromise park and to give maximum flexibility in its establishment. Written into the enabling legislation were certain measures which made it possible for the secretary of the interior and the National Park Service to take optimum advantage of the park opportunity and to get the biggest park possible for the money available.

In the nearly three years since the park was created, however, no advantage has been taken of these measures. No secretary of the interior has used the discretionary powers given him to intercede for the park. Three bureaus within the Interior Department—the National Park Service, the Bureau of Outdoor Recreation and the Bureau of Land Management—have been involved in implementing the park act, and none has assumed aggressive leadership. A master plan for the park's development is still not complete. The survey of park boundaries has moved at the pace of a banana slug, and the park boundaries are still not set.

And while the Department of the Interior has kept a respectful distance from the loggers, the loggers have not been so respectful of present or potential park values. They have proceeded forthrightly to "harvest" the great old giants that stand in areas which should be parkland and which members of Congress so stated specifically. The hole in Skunk Cabbage Creek, small in 1969, has now grown to a gaping wound: hundreds of acres in this exquisite area have been scraped bare. The chance to save even its glorious tatters diminishes day by day. Now logging is cutting deeper and deeper into areas above the Emerald Mile, and the sound of the chain saw can be heard at the Tall Trees Grove, where the tallest trees rise

EDGAR WAYBURN: *Road along Lost Man Creek*

from the flats of Redwood Creek. The logging trucks still rumble along Highway 101 bearing their unbelievable loads.

The Senate Interior Committee, concerned at the delays in implementing the Redwood National Park Act, scheduled "oversight" hearings in May, 1971. Testimony by National Park Service spokesmen suggested that development of the park might have to wait eight to ten years while Arcata and Georgia Pacific finish logging off areas which belong in the park, but would otherwise be blocked off by established park boundaries.

So the battle for the redwoods must continue. If new legislation is not forthcoming, and soon, even the fragmentary park we now have will be threatened. If logging continues along the present borders of the park, or even to the "buffer zone" proposed by some but not yet honored by the loggers, there will be three almost inevitable outcomes.

First, logged off areas upstream on Redwood Creek will fail to absorb and hold floodwaters in time of heavy rain. Torrents of water and gravel runoff will then topple the big trees in the park downstream, repeating the tragedy of Bull Creek when half a thousand giants went down like ninepins in one major storm.

Moreover, the scenic fringe of park trees along upper Redwood Creek will be a frail wall indeed if the forest behind them is logged to the present park boundary. Heavy storms and winds will subject this superb area to catastrophic blowdown.

And finally there will be no chance, ever again, to add great virgin groves to the only Redwood National Park on the planet.

The initial victory in the fight for a Redwood National Park, so dearly won, would then indeed be lost. The fight for the redwoods must be revived vigorously if we are to bequeath to those who follow us the heritage we have no right to deny them.

San Francisco, June, 1971

JAMES ROSE: *Lost Man Creek forest, logged in 1967*

EDGAR WAYBURN: *River-running, Redwood Creek*

As you enter the heart of Redwood Creek and the wild flow of life of its water, you emerge in another world.

You are a leaf on the water, your time here an instant in the timelessness of the forest.

JAMES ROSE: *Deer fern, Redwood Creek*

You drift in a realm of repose. The river reveals its full and changing beauty, the jewelled green of its waters, the moving tapestry of shadows and new forms around every bend.

You look, absorb, and meditate. There is a totality of existence here, a lovely intermingling of living things, a reassurance that life is meant to triumph, to continue unquenched.

JAMES ROSE: *Leaf pattern, Lost Man Creek*

You are the perfect visitor as you pass through this wilderness world.

You take nothing away but your own experience, your memory of the play of light on the moving waters and the great silent forests slipping by.

— PEGGY WAYBURN

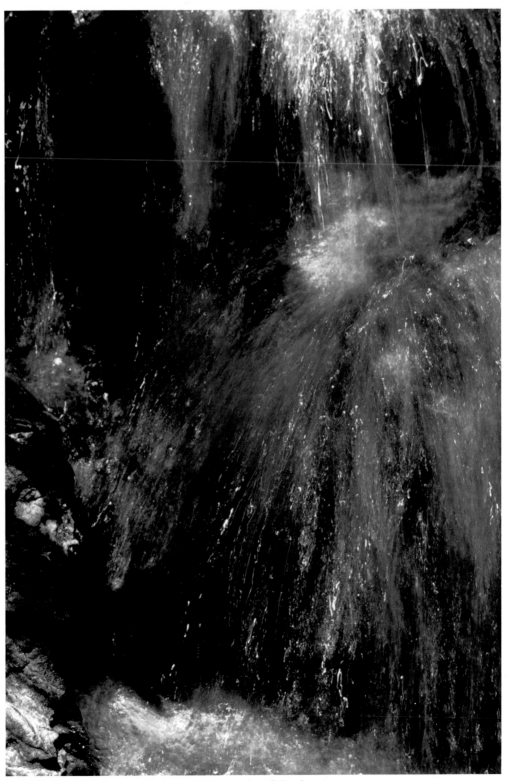

JAMES ROSE: *Cascade, the Emerald Mile, Redwood Creek*

DONALD ANTHROP: *Lower Redwood Creek*

It is fair to remember that
   this is not a land that belongs to us.
   We cannot destroy it without destroying something in us.
Its trees can teach us tenacity
   and patience and serenity and respect.
Life's urge to survive is the force
   that shaped them and their world of wildness,
   that made them one of the great miracles.

JAMES ROSE: *Forest detail, Redwood Creek*

Man, if he is too impatient to care,
can end this miracle, can terminate a chain of life
going back without interruption to an old eternity,

JAMES ROSE: *Unnamed prairie, Redwood Creek*

JAMES ROSE: *In Meditation Grove, Redwood Creek*

JAMES ROSE: *Grove in the Emerald Mile, Redwood Creek*

or man, able to create ideas, can meet his
old material needs with a different urge —
an urge to preserve what he cannot replace.

EDGAR WAYBURN: *Junction of Elam Creek and Redwood Creek*

MES ROSE: *Detail, Lost Man Creek forest*

Wildness made man but he cannot make it.
He can only spare it.
— DAVID BROWER

SPECIES LIST OF FLORA AND FAUNA

PAGE	COMMON NAME	SCIENTIFIC NAME
1	Coastal redwood*	Sequoia sempervirens
	Rhododendron	Rhododendron macrophyllum
5	Roosevelt elk	Cervus canadensis rooseveltii
7	Horsetail, scouring rush	Equisetum telmateia braunii
18	Miner's lettuce	Montia perfoliata (basal leaves)
20	Tanbark oak	Lithocarpus densiflora
	Iris	Iris purdyi
24	Bigleaf maple	Acer macrophyllum
30	Western five-finger fern	Adiantum pedatum aleuticum
	Mimulus, monkeyflower	Mimulus dentatus
	Montia	Montia sibirica
31	Blueblossom, mountain lilac	Ceanothus thyrsiflorus
	Rhododendron	Rhododendron macrophyllum
36	Red alder leaves	Alnus oregona
	Honey mushroom	Armillaria mellea
	Lovage	Liqusticum apiifolium
41	Sand verbena	Abronia latifolia
47	Brook foam	Boykinia elata
49	Sitka spruce	Picea sitchensis
51	Tree frog	Hyla regilla pacifica
55	Douglas fir	Pseudotsuga menziesii
59	Anemone, windflower	Anemone deltoidia
60	Sand verbena	Abronia latifolia
	Beach-bur (bottom)	Franseria chamissonis
61	Hazel catkins	Corylus californica
63	Wood fern	Dryopteris dilatata
84	Sword fern (right)	Polystichum munitum
	Hazel (along stream)	Corylus californica
99	Sword fern	Polystichum munitum
101	Five-finger fern	Adiantum pedatum aleuticum
	Brook foam	Boykinia elata
102	Licorice fern	Polypodium glycyrrhiza
103	Shelf fungus	Coriolus versicolor
104	Licorice fern	Polypodium glycyrrhiza
	Sword fern (foreground)	Polystichum munitum
105	Red alder	Alnus oregona
106	Moss	Epiphytic bryophyte
109	Sword fern	Polystichum munitum
111	Monkeyflower	Mimulus dentatus
	Starflower (center)	Trientalis latifolia
	Modesty (lower left)	Whipplea modesta
119	Buttercup	Ranunculus repens
124	Five-finger fern	Adiantum pedatum aleuticum
	Bigleaf maple	Acer macrophyllum (young tree)
129	Huckleberry	Vaccinium ovatum
	Bigleaf maple	Acer macrophyllum (in bud)
130	Sword Fern	Polystichum munitum
	Coastal Redwood branchlet	Sequoia sempervirens (with cone)
	Bigleaf maple leaves	Acer macrophyllum
134	Yellow bush lupine	Lupinus arboreus
147	Deer fern	Blechnum spicant
149	Leaves: red alder (center);	Alnus oregona
	Bigleaf maple	Acer macrophyllum
	Redwood sorrel	Oxalis oregana
153	Bigleaf maple	Acer macrophyllum
156	Horsetail, scouring rush	Equisetum hyemale californicum
159	Dogwood	Cornus nuttallii

* The coastal redwood—Sequoia sempervirens—is also shown on pages 3, 8–9, 12, 20, 22, 24, 26, 29, 35, 39, 45, 52, 63, 64, 74, 83, 84, 87, 88, 89, 92, 114, 118, 122, 129, 133, 136, 140, 142, 143, 144–45, 146, 152, 155, 157, and 159.